Everton: The Fans

Born, Not Manufactured

Published by Blue Horizon Press in 2022

Paperback ISBN: 978-1-7391061-0-2
eBook ISBN: 978-1-7391061-1-9

Cover design and typeset by SpiffingCovers

Everton: The Fans

Born, Not Manufactured

Bob Waterhouse

EVERTON FC HISTORICAL TIMELINE

1878 – St. Domingo Football club founded and club play in Stanley Park

1879 – Club renamed Everton

1880 – Everton join the Lancashire Football Association

1882- Everton move to Priory Road

1884 – Everton move to Anfield

1885- Everton turns professional

1888 – Everton join the inaugural football league

1891 – Everton win the Football League for the first time

1892 – Split of Everton FC and Liverpool FC – Everton move to Goodison Park

1906 – Everton win FA Cup beating Newcastle United 1-0

1928 – Dixie Dean's still record 60 goals in a season helps Everton win League for the third time

1933 – Everton win the FA Cup for the second time beating Manchester City 3-0

1939 – The team of Lawton win the Football League First Division

1948 – record attendance of 78,299 at Goodison Park for Liverpool derby

1951 – Everton relegated from Division 1

1954 – Everton promoted back to First Division

1961 – Everton appoint Harry Catterick as manager

1963 – Everton win the Football league First Division

1966 – Everton beat Sheffield Wednesday 3-2 to win the FA Cup

1970 – Everton win Football League Division 1

1971 – Ibrox disaster

1972 – Everton lose to Millwall in the FA Cup amid appalling scenes of hooliganism

1973 – Harry Catterick resigns

1975 – The Safety of Sports Grounds Act

1984 – Everton win the FA Cup beating Watford 2-0

1985 – Everton win the Football League and European Cup Winners Cup Heysel disaster in Brussels leads to ban of English teams from European competitions for 5 years

1987 – Everton win the Football league First Division

1989 – Hillsborough disaster and Taylor Report

1992 – Formation of English Premier League and Sky TV wins rights to show live matches

1995 – Everton win FA Cup beating Manchester United 1-0

2003 – Glazer takeover of Manchester United and Abramovich takeover of Chelsea

2008 – Sheikh Mansour takes over Manchester City

2010 – Fenway Sports Group takeover of Liverpool

2016 – Farhad Moshiri starts takeover of Everton

2021 – Failure of European Super League

INTRODUCTION

I wanted to write a football book on the history of my club that was different to all the others. I was less interested in the club's previous achievements and its great players than in examining the historical lifeblood of the club – its fans.

It's really important for the club to realise that what makes the club great, it's not the players, it's not the history, it's the people. – Neville Southall[1]

This book aims to understand and explain the social base of the supporters of Everton Football Club. In the past, they were the best supported club in the UK; in the 1963/64 season, during which I attended my first game, they had the highest average attendance in the old First Division – 49,401.[2] The book, although primarily focused on the fans of Everton, makes numerous comparisons and contrasts with various other clubs. It is hoped that it will interest not only the fans of Everton Football Club but also the supporters of all other football clubs.

Everton is a globalised club in terms of its owners and players. It also has fan clubs throughout the world. However, I want to explore whether its core support is still locally based for a club that has spent a record time of 118 seasons in the top flight. I wanted to examine the evolution of this foundation, explain its earliest local origins and how it has developed over the years. Despite living away from Merseyside since the age of eighteen, I have continued to follow the club avidly and have been a season ticket holder for the last three seasons. I regularly attend home games through my membership of Westcountry Blues, the official Everton fan club for the south-west of England. Although born on Merseyside, I have lived in the south-west for the last thirty-six years. Having made too many long trips up to Goodison Park by car from the south-west, I dithered about joining my local fan club that I'd kept seeing being advertised in the match day programme. Finally, after prompting by my youngest son, Henry, I finally joined the club in the late 1990s. This club is one that I now regularly use for attending matches and has even encouraged me to share a season ticket with Henry.

My early identification with the club certainly did not come from my family; my father was a rather lukewarm Liverpool supporter! It rather came from the community I grew up in and partly from the perspective of supporting the local 'top dog' of the day; Everton had just won the First Division championship in 1963 when I was first consciously a supporter at the age of six.

The purpose of this book then is to explore the history of Everton FC to gain a better understanding of its present support base. I would argue that the history of this founder member of the Football League mirrors many of the changes since the 1870s, such as broadening out its support base and developing foreign ownership, but does it also buck the trend by retaining more of its local support than other Premier League clubs? David Moyes first became manager of the club in 2002, and he got off to an excellent start in getting the fans on his side by describing Everton FC as the 'People's Club'.

"I was being driven into Liverpool, and for people who don't know Liverpool as a city, the kids are still on the streets playing football, the nights were just getting a little bit lighter.

"I saw all the kids on the streets playing football, but they were all wearing Everton strips.

"It just stuck with me – I said, 'the people on the streets of Liverpool support Everton' and I turned it into, it's The People's Club." – David Moyes[3]

I will explore whether there is still substance to Moyes' claim. I will examine the relative proportion of fans who live near to the club compared to other Premier League clubs. I will also examine the extent to which the fans have been affected by changes created by globalisation and whether their identification with the club has changed compared to more successful Premier League fans over the last thirty years.

This book intends to explain the history and development of this fan base, by looking at the early history of the club, and then explain its links with the current fan base. It will examine whether Everton is the Catholic club of Liverpool and whether its fans have a particularly local pattern of loyalty to the club. When I was growing up on Merseyside in the 1960s, there was a widespread belief that Everton was the Catholic club and Liverpool the Protestant club. I have even heard this view recently. For outsiders, it is worth bearing in mind that Merseyside has a particularly large Catholic community due to the waves of Irish immigration in the late nineteenth century. From being taken to watch Orange marches by my mother in the 1960s to experiencing the religious divisions in education, I was aware of the religious divide on Merseyside from a very early age.

The Orange Order is a 'fraternal' organisation, named for William of Orange, the Protestant Dutchman who seized the thrones of Catholic King James II back in the 'Glorious Revolution' of 1688. – BBC News 2012.[4]

Orange marches are associated with the Protestant community of Northern Ireland but also occur in Glasgow and Merseyside. However, as my Protestant school had a mixture of both Everton and Liverpool supporters, I was never really convinced of the religious segregation of football supporters on Merseyside. But the persistence of the belief among ordinary supporters made me want to explore it further.

The book is split between four main chapters. The first chapter explores the early history of the club from its initial founding by the St. Domingo's Methodist chapel in 1878 to the split with Liverpool FC in 1892 and its early days in the Football League. The second chapter explores the links between religion and football in the city of Liverpool and examines the widely held belief that Everton FC was supported mainly by the local Catholic population whereas Liverpool FC was predominantly supported by the local Protestant population. The third chapter focuses on the social background of the fans of Everton FC and how recent changes have affected this. The final chapter covers changes in football since the 1960s. There will be four distinct sections to this chapter – changes in the late twentieth century; changes in the twenty-first century; the development of a wider fan base; and the growing diversity of football fans following the Taylor Report which led to all-seater stadia and arguably encouraging more middle-class, female, ethnic, and gay fans. These changes will be constantly related to the fans of Everton FC. All chapters will also include comparisons and contrasts with other clubs.

I
THE EARLY HISTORY
OF EVERTON FC

Everton Football Club was one of many future leading football clubs to be formed against the background of rapid industrialisation and urbanisation during the mid to late nineteenth-century, Victorian period. Its fan base developed because of the large concentration of working-class people in the great industrial inner cities of Britain. Football became part of people's daily lives in the decades of the late nineteenth century when leisure time was gradually extended for manual workers.

> Within twenty years this free time was to be dominated by football in the winter months... – James Walvin[1]

Social historian James Walvin sees the attraction of football being encouraged both by late Victorian churches and schooling; the latter became compulsory at primary school level from 1870.

> Among the boys, the school football teams – and later the inter-school, inter-city, and even inter-regional school football competitions (themselves derived from public schools) – became of crucial importance in generating and maintaining the youthful commitment to football, particularly among working-class boys whose recreational opportunities were limited. – James Walvin[2]

As well as industrialisation, another key background factor linked to the creation of football fans were the Reform Acts of the nineteenth century which gradually gave the vote to the working class and created the party system which was ultimately crucial to the future split of the club into two; Everton FC and Liverpool FC.

The first Reform Act of 1832 abolished tiny districts and gave representation to the cities. Under growing pressure from the working-class Chartist movement, the 1867 act extended the vote to large sections of the male, industrial working class through enfranchising all householders and those paying over £10 in rent per year.[3]

> The 1867 Reform Act had, of course, extended the franchise, effectively ushering in the age of mass politics and, eventually, transforming the organization of political parties. The Act had given skilled and semi-skilled male artisans the vote and it appears that it was just that type of constituent who could afford the admission fee and leisure time to attend regular professional football matches. – David Kennedy and Michael Collins[4]

Politics drew upon existing social divisions; by the end of the century this largely meant social class. However, in the slightly earlier period, particularly in Liverpool, it was profoundly influenced by religion, not just between the large Irish Catholic population, who had recently escaped famine in Ireland, and the local Protestant population, but also between the Church of England and the growing Victorian Nonconformist churches. The latter term indicates that these churches were Protestant, but they did not conform to the doctrines of the Church of England. As will be seen later, the religious setting was important but did not lead to long-lasting divisions between supporters in Liverpool.

The football social historian Tony Mason has argued that the lack of manufacturing, and the dominance of casual work in the local economy, delayed the onset of football in Liverpool. Notts County, in 1862, predated the formation of Everton by sixteen years. However, he argues that the large number of clerical workers and the prominence of religion aided it.[5]

In the eighteenth century, John Wesley founded the Methodist church to directly communicate the gospel to ordinary people. In 1868, as part of the Wesleyan movement to encourage self-improvement among the industrial working class, the foundation stone for the Methodist New Connexion church was laid between two parallel roads near Stanley Park in Liverpool, St. Domingo Grove and St. Domingo Vale. It is worth emphasising that this move was not necessarily a success story of the mid-Victorian religious revival, as St. Domingo's replaced three other Methodist chapels whose congregations had slipped too low.[6]

One could speculate that the church's future encouragement for its young male congregation to become actively involved in sport was a recognition of the relative failure of its traditional religious practices to engage the participation of its urban, predominantly working-class parishioners. It was also part of the nineteenth century muscular Christian movement.

Muscular Christianity can be defined as a Christian commitment to health and manliness. Its origins can be traced to the New Testament, which sanctions manly exertion (Mark 11:15) and physical health (1 Cor. 6:19-20).
– infed.org[7]

Everton were one of many clubs to be influenced by this movement. Others included: Bolton Wanderers, Wolverhampton Wanderers, Aston Villa, Southampton, and Fulham.

Amongst the Anglican and Nonconformist ministry — and more especially in urban areas — there was great concern to provide leisure activities for their congregations. The move by the clergy towards the provision of sport was stimulated by the struggle by workers to shorten the working day through organisations like the Nine Hours Movement. Whilst advocating this shortening of the working day churchmen were concerned with the type of activities workers might pursue in their extended free time away from work. By the early 1870s the clergy had already moved to provide what they hoped would be alternative forms of attraction to the numerous public houses and beer houses to be found in urban areas. – David Kennedy[8]

By the end of the century, these methods seem to have secured a measure of success in the Everton district:

The dramatic fall in the proportion of Church of England worshippers in Everton was principally due to the increased presence of Nonconformists within the district. Nonconformists increased their presence from 19 per cent to 37.5 per cent of all those worshipping in Everton between 1851 and 1902. In 1851 Nonconformity's presence within the district was limited to just two chapels in the Everton Village area – one Baptist, the other Independent. By 1891 twenty-six chapels had been constructed and the presence of Nonconformity was widely felt throughout all areas of the district. – David Kennedy[9]

Both Everton and Liverpool football clubs evolved out of the Methodist St. Domingo football team that was set up by church members in 1878. The common origin of both teams is a significant factor in why religious-based football teams never evolved in Liverpool, unlike in Glasgow. This pattern of football clubs evolving out of local church teams, in the late nineteenth century, was matched by numerous others.

Writing in 2006, the writer on Christian influence on sport and business, Peter Lupson found that, of the then 41 clubs who had played in the Premiership, no less than 12 were formed in this way. Another club formed from a Methodist chapel was Aston Villa.[10]

The lack of a specifically Catholic team in Liverpool is in stark contrast to Scotland where Irish immigrants formed distinctively Catholic-based clubs[11]. According to the social historians David and Peter Kennedy, there is much evidence that Liverpool's Catholic leadership actively discouraged the development of such clubs[12]. I will discuss this in greater detail during Chapter 2 when the broader influence of religion on the fan base will be examined.

In 1877, young men associated with the chapel formed a cricket team. One of the first members of the team was Alfred Wade, son of St. Domingo's founder Joseph, owner of a coachbuilding business. Alfred would go on to become a director of the club. Henry Cuff was another trustee of the church whose son Will would become a player and future director of the club.[13]

However, the driving force in setting up the team was the minister appointed in 1877, Benjamin Swift Chambers. He was a Yorkshireman and a fan of cricket. In 1877, he managed to persuade the young men's Bible class to form a cricket team. A year later, he felt that the ground in Stanley Park would also serve as a football pitch, to give the young men an activity for the winter months.[14]

The initial attraction of cricket for Swift Chambers could have reflected the fact that, when Stanley Park was opened, in 1870 football wasn't played in England but was brought down from Scotland by unemployed Scots in search of work.[15]

The role similarly motivated clerics played in setting up future football clubs was significant at this time. The Anglican Tiverton Preedy played an even more crucial role in setting up Barnsley Football Club than Swift Chambers did in founding Everton. He became influenced by the muscular Christian movement through being at Lincoln Theological College with Edward Benson who had been at Rugby School when it founded the sport of rugby union. Preedy went on to help set up the football club after being disillusioned with the rugby team and seeing more potential to attract working-class players through football.[16]

In the late nineteenth century, it also emphasised faith in service to others over personal religious conviction and brought about a significant improvement in the quality of life of the poor and downtrodden.[17]

Another club whose formation existed due to the crucial role of a local church figure was Tottenham Hotspur. The person in question was John Ripsher, the Bible class teacher at the local All Hallows Church. Crucially, Ripsher was also a member of the Tottenham branch of the Young Men's Christian Association (YMCA). Boys from his Bible class had initially called the club Hotspur Football Club, because they had studied the exploits of Sir Henry Percy (Harry Hotspur) in their history class at school. Ripsher was the person the boys turned to in despair in 1883 after they had been the victims of bullying by older boys whilst playing matches on Tottenham Marshes. He formed a committee with him as president and treasurer which was to transform the club.[18]

As at Everton, the other big club on Merseyside at the time, Bootle was set up in 1879 through a curate at the local St. John's church – the Reverend Alfred Keely.[19]

As the St. Domingo club developed, public pressure gradually made the club not exclusively based on one Christian church.[20] The renaming of the club to Everton in November 1879 was part of this process. As the meeting was held in the Queen's Head pub, situated on village street at the historic middle of the Everton township, it seemed logical to call the club Everton.[21] The pub's landlord, J. W. Clarke, was a local Conservative councillor. Another outsider, notably the club's future president, John Houlding, was another local Conservative councillor. From his Stanley House overlooking the park, he observed the growing crowds attracted to the club and decided to get involved.

Houlding started out from humble beginnings, working as an errand boy and a cowman's assistant, before getting a job as a foreman in a brewery; this was the stepping stone to setting up his own brewery producing beers like 'Houlding's Sparkling Ales'.[22] The significance of this background was to play a major part in the future split which created Liverpool Football Club.

In 1880, the club decided to play in the Lancashire Football Association which had started in 1878/79. They were invited because the old Lancashire borders stretched that far south then, and they would gain support to develop football in the region.[23] According to Everton club historian Thomas Keates, they used their membership to become the most successful club in Liverpool.[24] Although they lost their first major Lancashire Cup match 8-1 against Great Lever FC in Bolton, they proved to be one of the most successful clubs in the league. This was boosted, in 1881, by the signing of ex-Rangers player Jack McGill. In the following season, the club's record signing played 22 times, winning 15 of those matches.[25] Partly because of these developments, the club's fan base rapidly increased. For the first ten years of the Football League, Everton had the highest average league attendance of any team in England. They recorded the first ever 10,000 plus attendance in the Football League against Accrington Stanley on 08.09.1888 at Anfield.[26] The potential of the club's crowds had previously influenced the first Football League to admit it into the group, even beating more established clubs like Darwen, Nottingham Forest and Sheffield Wednesday.

The seeds of the future split of Everton FC into two clubs were now sown in this following period, and this really is best understood by describing the long, drawn-out quest to find a permanent ground for Everton to play on. After four years of playing at Stanley Park, the club, in March 1882, decided to move to a piece of land in Priory Road owned by Mr. Cruitt which adjoined his house.[27] This move was the brainchild of John Houlding, who wanted improved amenities where the club could build hoardings, changing facilities and turnstiles. However, Everton were not granted home fixtures with leading clubs such as Blackburn and Bolton resulting in the club failing to make a profit. In his 2007 doctoral thesis at the University of Central Lancashire, Thomas Preston suggests that Everton were regarded by these clubs as 'minor and peripheral' due to the original football heartland being in Blackburn and Bolton.[28]

Two years later, Mr. Cruitt asked the club to leave his land, as the crowds became far too large and noisy, though Mr. Cruitt kept the fittings before the club's debt was paid off. This debt was eventually paid by two members of the Everton Committee. The Priory Road site, once bustling with eager football fans, is now covered with terraced houses.[29]

It was John Houlding that secured land at Anfield Road, owned by the Orrell Brothers brewery, which enabled Everton to move. This is the land that is now the current ground of Liverpool Football Club. In the 1880s, through a combination of wanting to do something for the public good and his growing commercial interests in owning a brewery and ten pubs, John Houlding had earned the nickname 'King John of Everton'. The ground was three hundred yards from one of Houlding's ten pubs – The Sandon Hotel. He also made himself indispensable to the club by loaning it £2,300 in the late 1880s which enabled it to erect covered stands, which ran the length of the pitch, and enclosures behind each of the goals. The stadium could now accommodate 10,000 spectators. By 1888/89, it could accommodate 20,000. It was the fans that directly led to the rapid development of the club.

On Merseyside during the late 1890s we estimate that average gate attendance at both Everton FC and Liverpool FC was about 10,000–15,000 each. By comparison, the constituency size of the largest local authority ward, also called Everton, was about 23,000, whereas inner city wards had fewer than 2,000 constituents in the early 1890s.

Undoubtedly, for local politicians an association with a soccer team that attracted the loyalty of a large number of fans offered the potential for media exposure to a big proportion of the local electorate. By the late Victorian period, ownership and management of a successful club could be an important political prize. – David Kennedy and Michael Collins[30]

The historian James Walvin has written about how the growth of mid nineteenth-century popular culture, of which football was an integral part, was encouraged by the gradual reduction of the working week, in particular the 'five-and-a-half-day' week created 'La Semaine Anglaise'. This was to provide the Saturday afternoon crowds which helped in the development of professional football. They had increased wages which they also spent on more regulated pastimes than had existed in the pre-industrial age such as boxing, animal baiting, and the turf.

Of all the recreational pursuits of the liberated working-class communities, none was more noticeable in its impact, more dramatic in its attractions (for both player and spectators) and more far reaching in its consequences, than the game of football. – James Walvin[31]

The club had also turned professional in 1885 which was crucial in Everton's invitation to take part in the first Football League in 1888. Everton were one of several northern clubs looking to turn professional at the time. This was despite the ban on it being imposed by the southern, public-school-dominated football association in 1882. Before the legalisation of professionalism, the northern clubs had players who had done a working week in industry.

> Clubs with working-class players did not want to see them to using up all their physical strength on a dockyard or railway during the week. – James Corbett[32]

After Preston North End, Great Lever and Burnley were expelled in 1884 for 'sham amateurism', such as paying players' wives or a nominee instead of the player, the FA were facing potential disintegration with a breakaway northern FA. Consequently, in 1885, the FA relented and allowed professionalism. Later in that year, Everton signed their first two professionals – George Dobson from Bolton Wanderers and Alec Dick from Kilmarnock.[33]

Everton had significantly higher crowds than Merseyside rivals Bootle. Some conspiracy theories, seeing Bootle as the strongest team on Merseyside at the time, have suggested that Everton won their position in the league due to bribery or Freemasonry. The Football League founder, William McGregor of Aston Villa, had a strict one city one club rule at the time which ensured that Bootle weren't admitted.[34] By 1891, the average crowd at Everton had risen to 11,000 – these were the largest for any club in the whole of England. A crucial factor in this was the relative size of Liverpool compared to the original hotbed towns of east Lancashire.

> The combined total of the 1881 populations of the other five Lancashire towns that provided original members of the Football League was still only 70 per cent of Liverpool's 611,000. – David Kennedy[35]

Consequently, they also took the highest gate receipts. This enabled the club to buy players like Alf Milward from

Marlowe in 1889 and several prominent Scottish players such as Alex Latta from Dumbarton, thanks to the ban on professionals lasting until 1893 in Scotland.[36] Houlding's role had been crucial in lifting the club to such heights.

His money and enterprise were largely responsible for the rise of Everton as one of the country's premier teams, from a city which by the 1890s had become the football centre of England. – James Walvin[37]

After an indifferent first season in the new Football League, the club finished second in the second year and eventually champions in 1890/91. They are also the only club from the original 12 never to seek re-election to the league.[38]

Up until 1893, the bottom four clubs of the Football League had to apply for re-election to it with Stoke City failing to retain their status first in 1890. From 1894-1921 it was the bottom three. From 1922-1957 it was the bottom two and from 1958-1986, after the formation of the old Fourth Division, all clubs coming bottom had to reapply. Southport, in 1978, was the last club to fail. After 1986, there was an automatic promotion set-up from the Conference, with winners replacing the club bottom of the Fourth Division.[39]

Everton never came bottom of the early Football League before the Second Division was formed in 1892, and they hold the record for the longest net time spent in the top flight of English football having only had four years outside of it.[40]

For the first ten years of the Football League, Everton had the highest average attendance ranging from an average of 7,260 in 1889 to 17,390 in 1898.[41]

Wishing to profit from his achievements in achieving these crowds Houlding sought an exclusive arrangement with the club to provide refreshments on match days. This led to many members of the board seeing an undue and commercial influence on club affairs, a situation that was exacerbated by Houlding's demand for a full remuneration of interest accrued from his loans to the club. Tensions were also increased when Houlding enabled a series of close supporters from his commercial and community dealings to become members of the board. Men like Thomas Howarth, William E. Barclay, Edwin Berry, John James Ramsay, and Joseph Williams would all continue to support him in the subsequent split of the club. – Thomas John Preston[42]

Houlding had already made himself financially indispensable to the club. In 1885, the owners of the ground at Anfield Road wanted to use the land for redevelopment which would have meant Everton Football Club being left homeless and most likely going out of existence.

Two of the committee were concerned and asked Houlding if he would buy the land to secure the future of the club. The cost was £6,000, a phenomenal amount at the time, worth £767,000 today, but Houlding was keen for the club to succeed. He understood Everton could not offer any promises financially and were only able to pay a rent of £100 each year. Generously, he accepted the terms on the understanding that when Everton could afford the going rate – £240 a year – the payments would increase.

He proposed Everton should buy his land, plus a plot adjoining it, and develop the facilities to cater for cycling and athletics and, therefore, secure year-round revenue. It was a visionary idea, but it did not succeed because the committee felt the price Houlding was asking for his land was exorbitant at a time when land prices were generally falling.

The committee remained open to paying rent for both Houlding's land and the adjoining plot but declined the option to buy. The adjoining land was owned by a man named John Orrell and he was asking £100 a year rent, while Houlding's plot had gone up to £250, meaning an annual outlay of £350 for the increased site.[43]

The club felt this hike, from what they had been paying, was too much and asked Houlding to reduce the rent on his land to £180 to reduce the overall cost. Houlding would not budge, instead reminding the committee of the agreement they had made in 1885.[44]

There is an alternative interpretation of events that Houlding's demands were a fair compensation and in line with the values of commercial loans of the times.

Overall assessment of whether or not Houlding's financial dealings with Everton were exploitative would depend very much on the yardstick used. It could be argued that the period of Houlding's involvement – and the financial backing he provided – was critical to the early success of the club when the game in the North was on the cusp of professionalization. If, though, the expectation is that early investors in professional football should not have received any financial reward, then Houlding failed to meet such a strict philanthropic threshold. However, by the standards of a more reasonable commercial criterion, there is no evidence of financial exploitation – he was a self-made businessman prepared to tie up a fair proportion of his assets in the promotion of a local football team, but one who expected modest financial rewards. – David Kennedy[45]

David Kennedy sees the main cause of the split to be Houlding's proposals, in 1891, to turn the club into a limited liability company. From his point of view, Houlding saw the club's future endangered by the potential development plans of John Orrell for land adjoining the perimeter of the ground and covering standing areas already erected. The new company would buy both Houlding and Orrell's land, thus securing the club's future. Houlding's opponents, who by this time constituted a majority on the board, viewed things differently. They wanted Houlding to agree a favourable rent for the land to continue the club's future. They also believed that, in the context of falling land prices, Houlding's proposals would mean that the club was subsidising him for his loss of land value.[46]

The rebels approached Orrell independently and managed to secure the land for £120 on a ten-year lease. Based on this agreement, which amounted to 2.5% interest on land valued at £4,800, they called on Houlding to charge a similar rate on his previous £6,000 purchase of the ground.

At a special general meeting in January 1892, when Houlding had refused these terms, most of the committee resubmitted their proposals and voted to form a limited liability company and move the club to another location which would subsequently be Goodison Park.[47]

Clearly, there is a lot more to the story than seeing Houlding as an exploitative landlord keen to cash in on the growing support of the club. Christian historian Peter Lupson also contends that there were broader political and moral divides between the two factions which will be partially examined in the next chapter. A significant number of the rebels were teetotal Liberals who were morally opposed to the activities of the Conservative brewer Houlding.

> The clash of values went beyond alcohol and money, however, branching out into politics. The committee members who were in the Temperance Movement were also active in the Liberal Party, which was wholly supportive of the anti-drink ethos. Houlding, however, was a Conservative councillor and at elections found some of the people he was sitting around the table with at Club meetings were opposing him politically at the hustings. People who Houlding proposed for key roles in local politics were being opposed by those who were his fellow committee members at Everton.

It would appear then, that while the disagreement over money and rent was at the centre of the feud, there were much deeper, longer-lasting tensions at play, stemming from a clash of moral values.

Quite simply, Houlding and the committee were destined to be at odds. Had he been a teetotal butcher, baker, or candlestick maker, it is entirely possible that the split would never have occurred and Everton may never have moved to Goodison Park. – Peter Lupson[48]

These local divisions need to be seen in the light of the national debate over alcohol. The passion of this debate may seem strange to contemporary views, however, in the late nineteenth century abolition was a key issue in the national political debate.

The timing of the dispute at the Everton FC coincided with a growing intensity in political agitation over the drinks issue at both national and local level, and political differences over the moral and social effects of alcohol were central to the dispute at the club. Through the 1880s agitation for reform of the licensing laws had become much more proactive. In particular, with refreshed evangelical zeal, the United Kingdom Alliance (established in 1853) galvanized opinion and lobbied hard for legislative change to restrict the trade in alcohol. The Alliance's official position was to support any political candidate that endorsed its policy of 'local veto' but, as another election approached in the early 1890s, the Alliance moved decisively closer to the Liberals. – David Kennedy and Michael Collins[49]

There was a particularly divided political atmosphere in the Liverpool of the 1890s when the club split into two:

The early 1890s was a period of significant change in Liverpool municipal politics, with the local tory ascendancy of over thirty years' standing facing a serious challenge from the Liberal party. For some years, unreformed ward representation and large-scale out-migration from the town had threatened the tories' hold on power, but it was the voters' concerns over the drink problem and over the efficiency and probity of the incumbent administration that provided the fiery substance of debate that swung the political pendulum towards the Liberals. – David Kennedy and Michael Collins[50]

This divided political atmosphere was clearly an important backdrop to the split, arguably more important than the widely held religious view of the break-up. The political consequences of the temperance debate were particularly strongly felt in Liverpool which had rates of crime and drunkenness offences way above the national average for the time.

Of the eighty-three temperance organizations officially represented at the 1884 National Temperance Congress, twenty-three had been drawn from a range of Christian groupings in the town and, by the late 1880s, Liverpool, along with Sheffield, was home to the most militant of the United Kingdom Alliance's local electoral associations. Vociferous in its attack on what it saw as decades of Conservative misrule, the Liverpool temperance movement transformed the city's social and political landscape. The respectable classes' anxieties about the disorderly and degraded social conditions of the inner wards ensured a receptive audience for the temperance message. – David Kennedy and Michael Collins[51]

It also needs stating that there is an alternative explanation for the split. Tony Mason quotes a contemporary *Liverpool Review* article at the time as describing the new Everton club as being 'Tory to the backbone' and puts the split down to Houlding's commercial instincts and power hunger.[52]

So how did Liverpool FC become a viable football club?

The first reason was that in John Houlding the club had an experienced chairman who loaned the club £500 to get started and arguably showed more financial expertise than the new board at Everton.

> Early Liverpool matchday programmes emphasise the commercial opportunities opened up to directors of the club. Advertisements for theatres and public houses with boardroom connections were commonplace in the programmes, as well as advertisements for brewing companies with shareholdings in the club. ... The difference in terms of corporate culture between Everton and Liverpool football clubs could not be starker. – David Kennedy[53]

Liverpool FC was formed as a consequence of John Houlding remaining as landowner of the Anfield Road stadium, and he was supported by a minority of the Everton board who were mainly his business associates. It was named Liverpool FC after Houlding first lost the legal right to continue running Everton FC.

Secondly, they possessed a first-class football facility in Anfield that needed no amendments to being accepted as a Football League stadium.

Thirdly, the rapidly expanding population of the city was able to support two clubs.

Finally, Houlding's previous experience at Everton was a key factor in enabling the club to be admitted to the new Second Division in 1893 which, after one season, became a vehicle for promotion to the top level. His appointed director

John McKenna applied for a vacant place in the new division after Accrington Stanley had resigned and Bootle couldn't afford professionalisation.[54]

As both clubs developed, they were dominated, not by the city's wealthy but, by the middle class, including clerks, managers, bookkeepers, and merchants. As for the fans, a survey for the weekly paper *Porcupine* in 1907 found that they were disproportionately better off, skilled and semi-skilled workers or middle class.[55]

I think that it would be a mistake to place the split of Everton into the two clubs firmly at the feet of the 'greedy' John Houlding. There were clear political and commercial differences on the old board of Everton which, in the context of late nineteenth-century England, made the break inevitable. Houlding was looking to make money from the club but, without his financial drive and vision, it is debatable whether the club would have taken off as it did to become founding members of the Football League.

The split of Everton FC in 1892, that brought Liverpool FC into existence, saw the emergence onto the football scene of a body of men with strong political identities. The men who controlled the fortunes of Everton and Liverpool football clubs also took an active part in local politics, and it would be strange, given the political environment these men operated within, that football in the city of Liverpool could have remained untouched from matters of religious controversy and discretely contained divisions in a purely sporting context. To understand why this would be so, it is necessary to take a short detour into the religiously divided history of Liverpool politics.

2
FOOTBALL AND RELIGION

Religious divisions on Merseyside were apparent to me from an early stage with the large Catholic population going to separate schools and me not having any Catholic friends. I only encountered Catholic children through playing football against Catholic schools such as Sacred Heart in Moreton and St. Joseph's in Wallasey.

By the time of my own upbringing on Merseyside in the 1960s and '70s, the conflicts of earlier in the twentieth century had appeared to have died out. However, I can remember the distress that my own mother felt one day after work when she had been shunned by the predominantly Catholic workforce in her dock canteen by inadvertently wearing an orange pinafore for the day on July 12th! What she had forgotten was that this was the date of annual celebrations by the Protestant community of the victory of William of Orange at the Battle of the Boyne in 1690. Although this was a much bigger event in Northern Ireland, it was marked on Merseyside by Orange marches. The fact that I was on the Protestant side and was an Everton supporter, as were many of my Protestant friends, didn't really convince me that the religious divide extended to football.

However, since the previously described split in 1892, there developed a widely held belief on Merseyside that Everton became the club of the substantial Merseyside Catholic population and Liverpool of the Protestant community. This belief was evident soon after the split and influential members of the clubs' respective boards seem to have given substance to this belief:

> While Everton was originally founded as a Methodist schoolboys' club, it has a strong lasting association with Merseyside Catholic Irish. The founder of Liverpool FC (originally called "Everton Football Club and Athletic Grounds company Ltd" or "Everton Athletic") was John Houlding, an Orangeman. So were most of the original directors including John McKenna. Houlding was a member of both the Working Men's Conservative Association and the Liverpool Protestant Association, the latter morphed into George Wise's Liverpool Protestant Party, which contested Liverpool Corporation wards Netherfields and St Domingo's as late as 1973.
>
> Everton acquired Catholic support ever since a certain Dr James Clement Baxter joined the board of directors at the turn of the 19th Century (also, the neighbouring Scotland Road and Vauxhall areas were, and continue to be, overwhelmingly Catholic). Obviously, Catholics were by no means the sole supporters of Everton (which commanded the support of most Liverpudlians), but it was noted nonetheless by many contemporary observers. Geography played, and still plays a part (The North-West versus South-East of the city), although this rejects the religious divide. – Dod[1]

The fact that many of the respective clubs' early board members were composed of influential, local politicians gave legs to this theory. This was particularly the case in a city which, at the time, had deep religious divisions often maintained by local political tensions.

The social historian David Kennedy sees the links between several of Liverpool's board members in the early twentieth century and the Liverpool Working Men's Conservative Association as particularly giving early weight to the football religious divide theory:

> The overlap of personnel between the Liverpool boardroom and the WMCA gives us further scope in understanding how perceptions of a sectarian football division between Everton and Liverpool could have taken root. Described as 'the engine of Protestant power' within Liverpool Conservatism, the WMCA were at the vanguard of anti-Catholic politics in the city.[2] – David Kennedy

The roots of religious divisions in Liverpool were created by the waves of Irish immigration to the city in the nineteenth century. The Irish potato famine of the 1840s was a particularly influential cause of the immigration as shown by the Irish medical historian Dr. Laura Kelly:

> The Famine had a devastating effect on the Irish population with 1 million dying from starvation and disease and, by 1855, a further 1.5 million had been forced to emigrate. Attracted by the prospect of work and relief through the English Poor Law system, considerable numbers travelled to the major towns and cities of the northwest of England. Lancashire, and in particular, the port of Liverpool, absorbed the greatest number of Irish emigrants because it was the primary destination for those leaving Ireland. Although migrants often arrived in Liverpool with the aim of continuing their journey to North America or Australia, many only had the resources for the first part of their journey. Others exhausted their fares for passage to America while waiting to depart, became too ill to travel, or fell victim to criminals who preyed upon their inexperience and exhaustion. – Laura Kelly[3]

Although in the early years there was a socially varied pattern of immigrants, after the 1860s there was a clear pattern of young, single, unskilled workers predominating:

> At times of peak employment, the Irish were recognised as being a crucial source of labour for the local economy in the north-west of England. Most Irish migrants worked in the worst-paid, lower classes of employment, surviving on a typical poor Irish diet comprised of potatoes, buttermilk and occasionally herring or bacon. In 1870, 82 per cent of Irish migrants in Liverpool were listed as unskilled manual labours, while 80 per cent of migrants leaving Ireland in 1881 described themselves as labourers, with 84 per cent of women describing themselves as domestic servants. Working in these spheres of employment, the Liverpool Irish were likely to have been more susceptible to the impact of trade depression, unemployment, and poverty.
> – Laura Kelly[4]

The Irish also became attracted to the city by the relative abundance of jobs, particularly those associated with the dock area. From 1835 – 1906 total tonnage of goods processed by the docks increased from 1,583,775 to 15,270,858.[5]

Also, during this time the population of the city doubled from 286,487 in 1841 to 746,144 in 1907.[6]

> The port of Liverpool became important in the development of the textile industry. By the beginning of the 19th century Liverpool had replaced London as the principal port where cotton was imported. To cope with this increased traffic, eight new docks were built between 1815 and 1835.

> The early part of the 19th century saw a rapid growth in the trade between Liverpool and Manchester. The success of the Stockton & Darlington railway opened in 1825,

convinced Liverpool merchants such as Joseph Sandars that the city needed a new transport system. Sandars formed the Liverpool & Manchester Railway Company and with the help of William James, recruited George Stephenson as chief engineer.

The Liverpool & Manchester railway was opened on 15th September, 1830. The railway was a great success. In 1831 the company transported 445,047 passengers. Receipts were £155,702 with profits of £71,098. By 1844 receipts had reached £258,892 with profits of £136,688. During this period shareholders were regularly paid out an annual dividend of £10 for every £100 invested.

The railway increased the importance of Liverpool as a trading centre. A new series of docks were built, including the Albert and Stanley Docks during the 1840s.
– John Simkin[7]

During the pioneering period of professional football in Liverpool, religious divisions dominated local life – affecting housing, schooling, and the city's occupational structure. By the mid nineteenth century, almost a quarter of the city's population were Irish born, and by the century's end Liverpool remained a key destination point for an exodus of Irish Protestants and Catholics.

Demographic research based on the 1881 and 1891 census figures illustrates the religious divisions in the city in the late nineteenth century:

These were maintained and reinforced by residential segregation in Liverpool in the mid to late nineteenth century. Indeed, each of the studies carried out at the Department of Geography at Liverpool University are quite clear in their portrayal of nineteenth-century Liverpool as a complex and differentiated urban landscape wherein each district had its distinct occupational, ethnic, and religious composition. Unskilled Irish Catholics predominantly populated the residential neighbourhoods adjacent to the north end dockland areas. Predominantly skilled manual workers (Ulster Protestant and Welsh nonconformist migrants) settled the heights above and to the east of the Parish of Liverpool. – David Kennedy[8]

Friction between the city's Protestant and Catholic populations was a feature of the social landscape – on many occasions erupting into street violence and rioting between the communities.

By the end of the nineteenth century, parts of Liverpool had become a bright and militant Orange, with the most partisan families living in Everton, Kirkdale, Edge Hill and the Dingle. Great Homer Street was the front line between Orange and Green. ... The Protestant Association, the National Protestant League, the Churchman's Council and the Layman's League were all founded with the sole aim of destroying Anglo-Catholicism and the High Church. – Andrew Lees[9]

Some historians have argued that the ferocity of the hostility between Irish Catholics in Liverpool and the 'native' British and Irish Protestant community was greater than the religious divide in Scotland and only stood in close comparison with the experience of towns in Northern Ireland:

Liverpool – sister of Belfast, rough, big hearted, Protestant and Unionist. Like no other mainland British city, Liverpool reflected the contours of the ongoing struggle in nineteenth century and early twentieth century Ireland between Unionism and Nationalism over the matter of Home Rule for Ireland. – David Kennedy[10]

These divisions in the city reached a peak in the city in 1909, just 17 years after the split between the two clubs and seven years after the death of John Houlding. On 20th June 1909, a proposed march from a local Catholic church near Scotland Road was attempted to be blocked by local Protestants. This led to several days of rioting. After the riots, an official government inquiry was set up which would run to almost 2,000 pages and which labelled Liverpool as 'the Belfast of England'.[11]

More recently, Wayne Rooney's grandmother has described him as 'Irish on the inside' and his legacy, as part of Croxteth's 60% Catholic community, is stressed as the continuance of the special links between Everton Football Club and the city's Irish Catholic population.[12]

As has already been described, the split between the clubs owed much to late nineteenth-century political divisions in the city. Uniquely in England, this split, well into the twentieth century, continued to have a religious aspect which was intimately associated with 'the Irish Question':

The important point to make here is that, whereas in other towns the issues primarily to be addressed and contested by local parties would be the more prosaic matters of, say, housing and health provision, or the setting of rates, in Liverpool "Imperial affairs" (that is, the stance taken by ward candidates on religion and the Irish Question), were paramount. For this reason it would be completely understandable, given the high incidence of football club directors active in the local Liberal and Conservative parties, if ethno-religious labels became attached to Everton and Liverpool football clubs via the politic views held by those directors. – David Kennedy[13]

Social historian David Kennedy has already shown how many early directors of Liverpool FC were officers in the Liverpool Conservative Working Men's Association; the

Glasgow Conservative Working Men's Association was also intimately involved in cementing the religiously separate development of Glasgow Rangers. He has also documented the similar influence of Freemasonry at the board level of both clubs. At the time, Freemason membership was barred by the Catholic Church. Not only was Houlding grand senior deacon of England, but in the first ten years of its existence, ten out of 133 directors and two club secretaries were Masons. This connection was maintained well into the twentieth century. The chairman and majority shareholder in Glasgow Rangers in the late nineteenth century, Sir John Ure Primrose, was also a leading Scottish Mason who used Freemasonry as a bonding agent within the club.[14]

Local blogger Dod claims that Everton acquired significant support in the neighbouring, predominantly Catholic, areas of Scotland Road and Vauxhall which was facilitated by the earlier role of Dr. James Clement Baxter, one of the new Everton's inaugural directors and a later chairman, who was a well-respected physician to many local Catholic families.[15]

The belief that the two clubs had a religiously based fan base, which was first developed shortly after the club's split in 1892, continued to be believed, up until the late twentieth century, of the religious divisions between the fans:

> People 'dressed' their houses then to advertise Cup final footballing allegiances, though my mum would never allow my brother's Evertonian blue to go up in case neighbours or passers-by mistakenly took us for Catholics – John Williams [16]

The late Eric Heffer MP (Liverpool Walton 1964-1991) once remarked he was obliged to associate himself with Everton FC (as opposed to the Protestant and formerly Tory-supporting Liverpool FC) throughout his career.[17]

...in Liverpool, even in two-ups, two downs, most Protestants were Conservative and most Catholics Labour, just as Everton was the Catholic team and Liverpool the Proddy-dog one. – Cilla Black[18]

Being a Roman Catholic school, religion played a large part in our school life. Pop Moran even tried to turn me off football at Anfield – Catholics were traditionally Everton supporters and players, Liverpool were the Protestant team. Pop honestly thought that being a Catholic I wouldn't be happy at Anfield – Tommy Smith (ex-Liverpool FC player and captain)[19]

The fact that Smith became a folk hero at Anfield suggests that these labels had no real substance even in the 1960s. However, as late as 2010, some commentators, like local historian J. P. Dudgeon, were still saying that Everton was the Catholic team and Liverpool was the Protestant team.[20]

However, my research, and most of the more detailed research, into the fans of Everton Football Club concludes that the religious divisions of Glasgow, and even to some extent Manchester, are in no way matched by football supporters in Liverpool. There, in fact, is overwhelming evidence to suggest that the fan base of both clubs is not based on religious divisions.

Although the Irish community had a flourishing amateur football league by the early twentieth century, this didn't translate into professional football. There wasn't the emergence of a Catholic club as was the case in Ulster, Glasgow, Dundee, and Edinburgh. Both clubs in Liverpool had emerged from the Methodist New Connexion chapel team of St. Domingo's.

When the club was renamed Everton FC, after the district where the renaming happened, the intention was to break the link with the Methodist church and broaden its support. Population research from the late nineteenth century indicates that the key factor attracting supporters with getting involved in the organisation of the club was the concentration of middle-class, clerical, and craft workers in the Everton ward. David Kennedy's research has found that most of the early shareholders came from this ward.[21] Although this ward was predominantly Protestant, the Scotland ward, where the biggest concentration of the Catholic population lived, was overwhelmingly composed of unskilled, manual workers who wouldn't have the money to invest in a football club.[22]

Although in 1913 Liverpool FC was criticised in the socialist press for not allowing a collection for striking Dublin transport workers, there is nothing in the local Catholic press of the time to denote a specific religious attachment in the pre-war years. Of the Irish national party councillors in the city at the time, Taggart had shares in Everton, while Austin Harford did in Liverpool.[23]

The question of why a similarly Catholic-based club, such as Glasgow Celtic, did not emerge in Liverpool is the key to understanding this issue. The detailed research of David and Peter Kennedy into this issue explains why this did not happen in Liverpool, even though Liverpool had the greatest proportional immigration of Irish in the late nineteenth century of any British city:

> ...in 1871 Liverpool had 15.45% of its population of Irish origin. The nearest to it was Manchester with 9%. – David and Peter Kennedy[24]

Crucially, the Kennedys have discovered that, despite the development of many Catholic football teams in the late nineteenth and early twentieth centuries, none of them developed into an equivalent of Glasgow Celtic. They have given two reasons for this. Firstly, none of the teams lasted or were part of an organised league. Secondly, the local Catholic leadership actively discouraged the development of such a team for their own political reasons:

It was the policy of the Liverpool Catholic hierarchy to integrate the Irish into British culture, whilst maintaining their Catholicism. This was due to the perceived threat to the native population of their poverty and passive support for Irish nationalism; to counter this the hierarchy tried to cultivate respectability through constructing a network of charitable organisations. It also tried to emphasise British, rather than Irish, culture in its schools. Also, Irish priests were vetted to screen out those with strong Irish nationalist views and 301 out of 391 priests employed were non-Irish. The leaders were outspoken opponents of Irish nationalism e.g. Bishop Goss was a stern critic of Fenianism, and Bishop Whiteside was actually a Unionist! The overwhelming loyalty was to the Pope, rather than to Irish nationalism. Many of their appointments to run Irish parishes were continental clerical orders e.g., the largest was St. Antony's on Scotland Road which was run by French missionary priests. The overall effect of this was to create specific parish, rather than Irish, identities. The parishes' sports teams played a full role in this. Irish nationalist politicians started to get elected in Liverpool by the late 19thc due to the development of universal suffrage. However, this seemed to direct them into developing the class, rather than ethnic, concerns of their constituents. The only MP to actively promote Irish nationalism in Liverpool was the Irish outsider Thomas Power O'Connor, who was criticised by local activists. – David and Peter Kennedy[25]

Indeed, as Everton and Liverpool football clubs progressed, they both developed strong links with both Catholic and Protestant populations. This was a stark contrast to Glasgow where both clubs only developed links with their own religion.

Both professional clubs fostered strong links with the Liverpool Irish. This was especially the case at Everton where some board members were influential supporters of the Home-Rule movement e.g., Irishman Dr. William Whitford, a surgeon, and Chairman of the Everton district Liberal association. A later Chairman James Clement Baxter, another prominent Liberal, was instrumental in securing the loan which enabled them to leave Anfield. His son, Cecil Stuart Baxter, also became Chairman of Everton. There were 2 other Liberal Home Rulers on the board – Alfred Gates and George Mahon. – David and Peter Kennedy[26]

At Liverpool, the initial period under the chairmanship of John Houlding gives support to the religious division thesis, as Houlding was a member of the Liverpool Orange Order and a prominent Mason.

However, after his death, evidence for this view rapidly eroded:

Three Irish publicans joined the board – John Joseph Hill, Thomas Crompton (a former Everton player) and William Harvey Webb. Even in 1892 there were Irish councillor shareholders in both clubs – John Gregory Taggart – Everton and Austin Harford – Liverpool. There is also strong anecdotal evidence that both clubs, but particularly Everton, gained strong support from the Irish community. – John Belchem[27]

Both clubs also provided facilities for teams of either religion to use, in contrast to Scotland and Northern Ireland. They have also both traditionally recruited from both backgrounds and supported local religious charities for both religions.[28]

In Scotland and Northern Ireland, ethnicity and religion strongly affected the development of football. In Scotland, there developed an antagonism to recruiting Catholic players by Protestant clubs as exemplified in the long-term, anti-Catholic discrimination at Glasgow Rangers. This only ended as recently as 1989 with their recruitment of ex-Celtic Mo Johnston.

In Glasgow, in stark contrast to Liverpool, games between the two main teams were a clash of cultures. Celtic originated from Irish Catholic immigrants and Rangers attracted much of their early support from native Protestant Scots who were opposed to the religion and culture of these immigrants.[29]

Like Everton, Glasgow Celtic was formed out of the church. But unlike the Methodist New Connexion, this church was the Roman Catholic church. A Catholic priest in the east end of Glasgow, Brother Walfrid, originally formed the club as a fundraising organisation for three east end Catholic parishes to stop the Catholic poor from being tempted into apostasy by going to Protestant soup kitchens.[30]

Religious divisions became entrenched in 1912 when the Belfast shipbuilders Harland and Wolff set up a yard within walking distance of Ibrox. They imported a Belfast Orange workforce and only recruited Protestant workers.[31]

Rivalry between the two Glasgow clubs often led to violence, even in the early twentieth century. This has rarely been the case in Liverpool. Liverpool FC historian Steven Kelly documents a long history of good relations between the fans of both clubs which slightly declined in the 1990s.[32]

Plenty of other factors, not replicated on Merseyside, also ensured that the pattern of local rivalry would be different. The Church of Scotland was a strict brand of Calvinism, based on John Calvin's belief that only some are chosen to be saved by God, which fiercely rejected Catholicism and had largely obliterated it from all but the most remote parts of Scotland. Consequently, Catholicism was specifically associated in Scotland with the immigrant Irish population living in Catholic ghettos. This tended to reinforce links with Ireland which the colours and emblem of Celtic represented. Both clubs maintained strong links with the Catholic Church on the one hand, and the Orange Order on the other. They have also supported Catholic causes over the years, e.g. 1949, 27,000 attended Parkhead to celebrate the centenary of Catholic young men's societies and 1978 hosted the centenary of the restoration of the hierarchy. Rangers, for many years, offered use of ground to the Orange Order for an annual service before the marches of 12th July.[33]

As has been previously described, these links were never really developed in the first place in Liverpool. The clubs developed in a very different way to those of Glasgow:

> Issues of Catholic identity or Irish Republican politics, or Loyalism and Protestantism are insignificant to the vast majority of Liverpool and Everton supporters. Cultural, religious, and political assimilation has occurred in the city and the repudiation of sectarian associations by its main clubs has been an important part of bridge-building and the dilution of older animosities. – Keith Daniel Roberts[34]

In Northern Ireland, the establishment saw football as a vehicle for Unionism, and Linfield FC, the biggest club, became identified with the Protestant cause. There was also discrimination to Catholic clubs from the football authorities who sometimes found it difficult to join local and regional leagues. Belfast Celtic's fixtures were often marked by crowd violence. It was eventually forced out of existence due to this in 1949. They had played in the traditional Boxing Day fixture with Linfield when, after Linfield scored a late equaliser, Linfield fans invaded the pitch and badly attacked several Celtic players. After feeling that the response from the Irish Football Association was totally inadequate, it withdrew from the league.[35]

Local journalist Frank Curran later commented:

> 'Belfast Celtic knew it wasn't a football problem, and that there was nothing they as a football club could do to end it. So, they got out.'[36]

By contrast in Liverpool, Irish teams seemed to face little or no hostility in being admitted to local leagues. Both clubs provided players to train the St. Francis Xavier club team. There also seems to have been free movement between local club teams, e.g. St. Francis Xavier and Britannic. The lack of hostility was maybe also due to the absence of an Irish threat to the two major clubs.[37]

One of the more recent developments, that gave rise to the view that Everton is the Catholic club, was the significant recruitment of Irish Catholic players by the club in the 1950s:

> Through the 1950s, the Everton team took on a distinctly Irish flavour, with the likes of Peter Farrell and Tommy Eglington becoming big crowd favourites. This brought about a significant influx of Irish fans and may have been responsible for suggesting a Catholic flavour. – Michael Kenrick[38]

However, this seems to be due to Everton's more extensive scouting network in southern Ireland than to any religious link. Indeed, there seems to be no evidence that either club deliberately targeted a particular community in their recruitment policies:

> ...despite there being a marked difference between Everton and Liverpool in the volume of players selected from Ireland, evidence suggests that, overall, there was no attempt by the clubs to operate discriminatory policies on the grounds of religious sectarianism when employing playing staff. And neither does there appear to have been any policy to build up support amongst one section of the population to the detriment of attracting support from another section. – David Kennedy[39]

In Manchester, there is more historic evidence of a footballing religious divide which could arise from Manchester City's origins in the Church of England parish of St. Mark's in Gorton and Manchester United not arising from the same source. The club developed through the work of Anna Connell, daughter of the vicar of St. Mark's, the Church of England church. She wanted to do this to tackle crime and drink among the workers in a rough, working-class district in the east end of Manchester.

Initially, she set up weekly talks, music, and singing. But, inspired by a meeting with William Beastow, a senior official of the Union Iron Works and a linesman at the church, she proposed the formation of a cricket team in 1879. The following year, this was widened to include a football team. When they moved next to Belle Vue showgrounds ironically their first game was against Newton Heath, later to become Manchester United. In 1884, they merged with Gorton Athletic and changed name to Gorton. In 1887, following another move, they were renamed Ardwick AFC. Like Everton, it was strongly influenced by a brewer, Stephen Chesters Thompson, who, with another wealthy businessman, John Allison, wanted to invest in, and develop the club. Consequently, they started recruiting professionals from Bolton Wanderers and Scottish clubs. This eventually led to them becoming founder members of the Football Alliance in 1891/92 that became the Second Division the following season.[40]

Manchester United arose out of railway workers of the Lancashire and Yorkshire depot at Newton Heath. At the inception, it was a club for the whole workforce, not just the Catholic ones. However, when it moved to Clayton, from 1893-1910, it started to attract the support of the local Italian and Irish population. One of the former, Louis Rocca eventually became the club's chief scout and wanted the club to be renamed Manchester Celtic in 1902. When they moved to Old Trafford, in 1910, they attracted the heavily Catholic support of the local Salford dockers.[41]

In the 1930s, Rocca set up a network of Catholic scouts

and is credited with bringing Glasgow Catholic Matt Busby to the club. Busby's right-hand man, Welsh Catholic Jimmy Murphy nurtured many Irish Catholic players like Jimmy Carey and Shay Brennan. Busby was also replaced with three subsequent Catholic managers – Wilf McGuinness, Frank O'Farrell, and Tommy Docherty.

The recruitment policies of Manchester United were also focused earlier on Southern Ireland when they became the first club to sign an Irish player in the early twentieth century. Their widespread recruitment of Catholic players in the 1950s also led to some of their Protestant professional players to complain of discrimination against them.[42]

However, the fact that Protestant Irish players like George Best and Sammy McIlroy were also recruited, and that their most successful manager, Alex Ferguson was also Protestant, tends to undermine the view that United is a Catholic club.[43]

Another anecdotal contradiction to the football religious divide view is the common experience of many families on Merseyside having split footballing loyalties. In the 1980s, it was also common for fans of both clubs to travel to Wembley Cup Finals together when facing each other. However, there are some signs that this has evolved over the years. When speaking in the1970s, the then Liverpool Chairman, John Smith, who came from a brewing background, explained:

> Twenty years ago, I wouldn't have dared put a Catholic in to manage a pub in a Protestant area. Liverpool could have gone the same way as Belfast, or Glasgow, over religion. But when you've got streets, offices, and shops, even families divided down the middle-Red or Blue-they haven't the time or energy for other divisions. – Brian James[44]

It must be said that the religious football divisions are also breaking down in Glasgow.

Both Glasgow clubs are changing due to changing fan base and changing world. Celtic is engine for change under its Chairman Fergus McCann. Under him there is a new club mission statement – 'to maximise all opportunities to disassociate the cub from sectarianism and bigotry of any kind. To promote Celtic as a club for all people regardless of sex, age, religion, race or ability.'

He gained control of Celtic in 1994, with only eight minutes to go before the company was to be declared bankrupt.

He spent £41 million rebuilding ground and £40 million on players. This led to season ticket holders increasing from 8,000 to 53,000. Has also appealed to emerging middle-class support who don't relate to sectarianism. Has encouraged groups like 'Bhoys against Bigotry' to change attitudes of fans and to instil a new sense of tolerance.[45]

Also, although some areas of Liverpool such as Scotland Road and Vauxhall were predominantly Catholic, there were no equivalents to the exclusively Catholic ghettos in the east end of Glasgow.[46]

By the late twentieth century, even these predominantly Catholic areas in Liverpool, and other predominantly Protestant areas such as the Netherfield Road, were broken up by slum clearance and a move to new housing estates on the outskirts of the city such as Netherton and Kirby. These developments, along with the general decline in religion, the growth of mixed marriages, and the loss of interest by younger members were seen by local historian K. D. Roberts as the main reasons for the decline of the Orange Order in the city. He also concludes that the pattern of slum clearance was crucial to the breakdown of religious divisions. Although there was significant slum clearance at the turn of the twentieth century, the vast majority was in the mid twentieth century. At the end of this process, there were few remaining anecdotal references to support the religious divide for both teams.[47]

Approximately 161,000 people, almost one-third of Liverpool's population, were 'forced to leave' the city.55 In the Liverpool Scotland constituency alone the electorate fell from 56,000 people in 1955 to 25,000 people in 1971.56 One of the main areas of resettlement was Kirkby, whose population had already exploded from 3,000 to 52,000 in the space of ten years, by 1961.57 Kirkby's population, however, was set to swell again. A report from the *Liverpool Daily Post* in 1957 mapped out the 'Blueprint for Exodus': 30,000 more people would head for Kirkby, 48,000 people would go to Skelmersdale, 18,000 to Widnes, 19,350 to Halewood, 6,000 to Cantril Farm, and 3,500 to Formby.58 Tens of thousands more would relocate in Runcorn, Ellesmere Port, Winsford, and within the city in areas such as Norris Green and Speke.59
– Keith Daniel Roberts[48]

This contrasts greatly with Glasgow. A report by Glasgow City Council in 2003, showing that 5% of their survey were afraid to go into some parts of the city due to their religion, suggests that its housing policy hasn't had a similar impact on the decline of religious-based housing. This survey also found that 75% believed that religious divisions remain.[49]

The 1960s was also an era of relative affluence in Liverpool which allowed both communities to forge a common identity following the developing 'Merseybeat' sound or following the city's football clubs.[50]

By the end of the 1960s, Liverpool became a Labour stronghold after years of supporting the Conservatives, aided by the Protestant working class, influenced by the Orange Order, voting Conservative. An earlier development was the Catholic working class moving to Labour from Irish nationalism in the 1920s.[51]

In the late twentieth century, the common experience of economic decline and unemployment gave both communities a shared experience which led to a growing hostility to Conservatism. The Conservative Party lost its last Liverpool City Council seat in 1994 and its last parliamentary constituency in 1983.

> Later, as the century progressed, the political alternatives people were adopting meant that, amid the city's dramatic economic fall, the focus had moved onto 'a bigger enemy' than neighbours of a different religious persuasion. – Keith Daniel Roberts[52]

This transfer of political support reflects a decline in religious divisions which have also been mirrored by the two city football clubs never developing lasting religious loyalties.

The overwhelming amount of research evidence indicates that neither Everton nor Liverpool football clubs, despite their origins, has a specific, religious-based support on the lines of clubs in Scotland and Northern Ireland. As the research of David Kennedy suggests, the greater impetus in creating the separate clubs was political, rather than religious.

This, essentially nineteenth-century political divide between Liberalism and Conservatism, rapidly declined in the twentieth century, and there is no evidence that the subsequent Labour/Conservative divide was matched by the footballing division in Liverpool. What is remarkable about the division of football support in the city, given the city's historic links to religious divisions, is how little they have been influenced by these links.[53] In 1985, Tony Mason found that, among the fans, there was some uncertainty as to which club was associated with which religion. Decisions on which club to support came from a plethora of individual preferences, rather than having a clear social element.[54] Perhaps the greatest argument against the myth that Everton is a Catholic club is the existence of the Church of England St. Luke's church in one corner of the ground. More recently, the late church chaplain Harry Ross developed particularly close relations with the club:

Over the years the church has formed a close bond with its footballing neighbour. Reverend Harry Ross, parish vicar from 1977 to 2010, was officially appointed as club chaplain in 1994 and became a leading figure in the Everton Former Players' Foundation. ... For many fans, both home and away, a visit to St Luke's forms part of the Goodison pre-match ritual. Church volunteers welcome supporters and emergency services in the parish hall where tea, coffee and sandwiches are served. Upstairs, the EFC Heritage Society lays on an array of magnificent displays and stalls as well as hosting collections for the KitAid charity. In 2016 the church came to national attention when the BBC's Football Focus was broadcast live from the hall before an FA Cup tie against Chelsea. – Rob Sawyer[55]

The common origin of the Methodist church and the markedly non-religious-based policies of both clubs have ensured that the religious/football divide in Glasgow has not been matched in Liverpool. Also, the city of Liverpool developed a non-religious-based local culture earlier than did Glasgow.

Arguably, football itself has played a huge part in ending sectarian divisions in the city:

'...in the end football did probably more for unification in the city than either the church or the city's politicians.' – Andrew Lees[56]

'... In their very first game against new rivals Everton, the newly named Liverpool FC fielded nine Irish Glaswegian 'Macs' from both sides of the religious divide who looked "as likely a lot of raw-boned Scottish laddies as ever skipped over thistles". In the early years, all the board members of both clubs were staunchly conservative with a Scottish Methodist work ethic, and they maintained close links with one another. Every Saturday afternoon, the children of men who had sought refuge in Liverpool arrived in droves to cheer on their team and their adopted city by the sea. Migrants looking for a new identity who had torn free from their roots to forge a different life in a strange place joined them in what became an unbreakable union of solidarity. – Andrew Lees[57]

Today, it's the norm for families to be divided, as mine was with my Liverpool-supporting father. This has been graphically illustrated by Keith Daniel Roberts when he quotes the letter sent by Evertonian Steve Rooney to *The Guardian* journalist Geoffrey Wheatcroft, and complete Merseyside outsider, who had written in 2004 that, bizarrely, Everton was a Protestant club and Liverpool a Catholic one:

My own predominantly Catholic family has always been split between Red and Blue. Likewise, there are plenty of big Protestant families who are similarly divided in their support for the two clubs. One of the reasons that Everton and Liverpool have, mercifully, been able to maintain a relatively healthy, and for the most part friendly, rivalry is precisely because – unlike Glasgow – our footballing allegiances are in no way rooted in divisive sectarian religious differences. – K. D. Roberts[58]

I could make the same comments about my wider Protestant family which contains both Liverpool and Everton supporters. Most of my cousins, who follow football, tend to support Liverpool. This reflects my own strong view that football in Liverpool does not reflect the historic religious divide in the city. This is, despite the fact, that many Everton fans do sing songs with apparently religious inspired lyrics such as – 'To hell with Liverpool and Rangers too, we'll throw them all in the Mersey' to the tune of 'The Irish Rover'. However, there is recent evidence that the lyrics were not inspired by religious division but rather fighting between

Everton and Rangers' fans after their 'Battle of Britain' match in 1963.[59]

The breakdown of any possible religious divisions between the clubs has also been helped by developments in football since the 1960s including: the development of the English Premier League and UEFA Champions League; the evolution of a wider fan base following the expansion of satellite TV and social media coverage which has led to a globalised support of English football; and the evolution of a more diverse fan base in the aftermath of all-seater stadia and the growth of women's football and football's efforts to attract gay and ethnic minority fans. All these issues will be explored in relation to Everton FC fans in the last chapter. But first I will have a look at the club's current fan base.

3
EVERTON FC AND ITS FANS

When I was attending Barnston Lane Primary school in Moreton just over seven miles from the city centre, it was unusual for anybody to support a club other than Liverpool or Everton. We all duly turned up to football practice in our respective club shirts. I only knew one boy, Christopher Chaloner, who supported Manchester United and that was because his dad was from Manchester. We all had a tremendously local affiliation to our respective teams which have continued to be among the best supported in English football.

Everton have a large fan base by virtue of being an original founder member of the Football League and contesting more seasons in the top flight than any other club. For the first nine seasons in the Football League Everton had the highest average league attendances of any team in England. [1]

The highest ever season average attendance at Everton was in 1963, with 51,603, the best of any club in that season. The following season, the club was once again the best supported side in England, and this was the first season that I saw an Everton fixture. I was part of the 49,504 crowd that saw us beat Blackpool 3-1. My dad drove through the Mersey Tunnel in his recently acquired grey Ford Anglia to be confronted with hordes of local youngsters demanding money to 'protect the car'. Realising that these kids were significantly rougher than my Wirral schoolmates, he wisely decided to comply. It was at this match that we got into a routine of buying a bag of Nuttall's Mintoes and paying for seats in the Gwladys Street Upper Stand, which is still there today. I can't remember the two goals by Fred Pickering and the one by Alex (The Golden Vision) Young. What I can remember was the passion of the crowd, which my dad didn't share at all, and being hooked. For the next six seasons, my dad reluctantly accompanied me to the regulation three or four matches per season that he could tolerate. They tended to be matches against lesser opposition, as Dad wanted a reasonably quick exit, so results were usually favourable.

In recent times, average attendance has slipped to averages in the late thirty thousands. This is, to some extent, a reflection of the move to all-seater stadia, but also reflects the relative decline of the club. However, at the end of the 2016/17 season, the club announced that every home fixture had been a sell-out and all season tickets for the following year had been sold out.[2]

One aspect of this loyalty is the club's peculiarly local fan base. The 2004/05 Premier League survey, which asked almost 1,400 Everton fans various questions, found that 40% of match day fans lived within 10 miles of Goodison Park. In my childhood, our house was comfortably within this radius. Today, I am part of the growing 60% living over 240 miles away in Dorset. Altogether, 77% of Everton fans lived less than 49 miles away from the stadium.[3] The 2007/08 survey found that, on average, Everton fans lived 44 miles away from Goodison Park, 3 miles less than the average and a huge difference compared with rivals Liverpool and Manchester United who were 82 and 78 miles respectively from their stadiums.[4] A similar survey in 2002 found that 73% of Everton fans were locally born compared with 57% for Liverpool and only 43% for Manchester United.[5]

Everton's experience of a local fan base stands in stark contrast to a club like Chelsea whose locality has undergone a huge gentrification (becoming middle class) for over, at least, a fifty to sixty-year time period. In 1998/99, one survey indicated that two thirds of Chelsea season ticket holders lived outside of London.[6]

The contrast between the localities of Chelsea's Stamford Bridge and Everton's Goodison Park could not be greater. Stamford Bridge lies in the Parsons Green and Walham ward of the Hammersmith and Fulham borough. The council description of this ward is:

> The ward is [a] very affluent area. The overall population is middle-aged and young, single, healthy and skilled. A high proportion of the population work in well paid professional jobs mainly in scientific and technical or financial and insurance activity sectors. – Hammersmith and Fulham Council[7]

The research of geographical blogger Alasdair Rae tells us that over half of Premier League clubs have their grounds in areas among the bottom 20% most deprived in the country.[8] Everton not only is on this list but the County ward, in which the Everton ground is situated, is the second most deprived ward, in one of the most deprived cities, in the country.[9]

It is obvious, when walking around the ground, that it is situated in a deprived area. This is more through observing the shuttered-up shops on Walton Road rather than the usually well-maintained terraced houses that closely surround Goodison Park and all four sides that make expansion and modernisation of the ground impossible.

> Everton draws the vast majority of its support from Merseyside, Cheshire, Lancashire, and North Wales. However, Everton's support heartland is traditionally based in the North-West of the city and in the southern parts of Sefton. Although no conclusive studies have been undertaken, supporters are more prominent in areas such as Aintree, Anfield, Bootle, Croxteth, Everton, Kirkdale, Vauxhall and Walton with the northern parts of Liverpool seen as Everton dominated. – Wikipedia[10]

Everton's local nature of followers has also meant that it attracts support from some of the poorest electoral wards in the country. In the 2019 'Indices of Deprivation' report, Liverpool had the second highest number of areas in the most deprived 10% nationally.[11] There was a particularly high concentration in the North Liverpool heartlands of Everton's support. This means that Everton still has a core fan base rooted in the traditional working class having a significantly lower income than average fans.

The Premier League National Fan Survey of 2003/04 backed this up by showing that the club had the highest percentage of fans in the lowest income brackets with 71% of Everton fans earning under £30,000 a year.[12] I can remember Tottenham fans flashing £10 notes toward Everton in the ground ten years before the advent of Harry Enfield and his famous 'Loadsamoney' character.

In the previous year, the Sir Norman Chester Centre for Football Research survey found that 30% of Tottenham Hotspur, and 32% of Chelsea supporters, earned over £50,000 a year which the survey calculated was the wealthiest bracket.[13] One consequence of deprivation is the relatively cheap prices in the pubs around Goodison Park. I have recently witnessed Chelsea fans ordering rounds of beer with £20 notes at Wetherspoon's on County Road and greeting their mountains of change with the immortal words – 'You're havin' a larf'!

More up to date research by footballtips.com puts average Everton supporter wages at £23,000 per year – 16th out of 20 premiership clubs. The same survey put Brighton fans top with a wage of £43,000 and Chelsea second at £41,000.[14]

The Premier League National Fan Survey of 2002/03 report found Everton had the highest number of season ticket holders from the two lowest social classifications with 16%, which was 1% more than Sunderland.[15]

A study, in August 2012, by property website Zoopla found that houses around Goodison Park were the cheapest of any Premier League club averaging £66,000, almost £30,000 less than 19th placed Villa Park with £94,000. Chelsea's Stamford Bridge came in highest with average house prices of £1,467,000.[16]

It waits to be seen how far Everton's move to a new ground will stimulate house prices in the Bramley-Moore Dock area. However, since Farhad Moshiri's takeover of the club in 2016, there has been little sign of a boost in property prices around the ground. There is some research to suggest that both developments could have some impact. Ahlfeldt and Kavetsos found a rise in property prices near to the new Emirates (Arsenal) and Wembley stadia in London.[17]

In 2011, and in 2020 when assessing the impact of a possible Saudi takeover of Newcastle United, the property firm StripeHomes released research that it could have a positive impact on local property values:

> The research shows that house prices benefit from big name takeovers with 5% in the first year and 15% in three years. This article was widely spread in the British (real estate) media. According to the managing director of StripeHomes, a takeover of Newcastle by the Saudi's will cause a rise in house prices because it puts the city on the map. – Jelmer de Visser[18]

However, the same research found a negative effect of 11% from the takeover of Manchester City on local house prices.[19]

When David Moyes became the club manager, in 2002, he described Everton as the 'People's Club'. As well as an inspired way of getting the fans on board, Moyes's observations that Everton seemed to have more fans living in the city than Liverpool was a shrewd observation of Everton's particularly localised fan base. It must be said that there was precious little factual evidence to make such an observation and certainly there is evidence to the contrary. In Everton's own 2019 city survey, to support their planning application for a new stadium, the survey sample contained twice as many Liverpool fans as Everton. Admittedly, the sample size of 2,000 is very small and not guaranteed to be representative. However, the document also states that the survey split was also what was expected throughout the city.[20]

Everton Football Club has rightly won huge respect for its pioneering work in its local community. The Everton in the Community charity promotes health, education, social inclusion, and equality of opportunity programmes to over 30,000 people throughout Merseyside and North Wales. Indeed, in the Premier League National Fan Survey for 2014/15, it indicated a particular pride in the unrivalled work that the club does in the local community with 91% indicating that it was an important part of the club's culture and philosophy.[21]

This charity programme stands in stark contrast to many other club programmes that have not always been as successful.

Many clubs struggled to reach out and make links with their increasingly diverse neighbours. When they did so, the initiative often came from external governmental agencies or the influential Professional Footballers' Association (PFA). This was true of the 'Football in the Community' schemes which began in the mid-1980s and encouraged clubs to open their facilities to 'community use' and appoint 'community officers'. Some have been rightly criticised for failing to probe beyond the public relations and marketing advantages of such schemes to engage in any meaningful sense with the communities around them. – Matthew Taylor[22]

In 2018, Everton in the Community celebrated thirty years of their community work. In this time, they have aimed to tackle key social issues to create stronger communities and help some of the more vulnerable in the Merseyside region.

Recognised as one of the most progressive sporting charities in the world, EitC improves the lives of 20,000 people every year and supports more than 1,100 children through school sports programmes. More than 1,000 residents have also been helped back into work thanks to their employment support, while, in 2017 alone, over 100 young people graduated from the charity's apprenticeship programme. – LiverpoolExpress[23]

The football journalist Henry Winter has also described Everton's community work in particularly glowing colours compared with other comparable clubs:

All Premier League clubs are involved in community work but few do it as well as Everton... – Henry Winter[24]

He also documents the club's social inclusion schemes confronting racism and homophobia. They have been particularly applauded for their work with the homeless with many players even volunteering to sleep rough for a night.[25] In 2019, Winter wrote about a man, not even from the Merseyside area, who walked into the club's community hub near Goodison Park as he knew that the club helped the needy and he did not know where else to go![26]

In 2018, Everton in the Community was granted local recognition by being given the freedom of the city of Liverpool.[27]

There are countless examples of other individuals who feel indebted to the club including Lance Corporal Dave Curtis, who was helped to cope with post-traumatic stress disorder and claims that:

'Everton in the Community saved my life' – Premier League.[28]

On the same theme, in November 2021, another fan felt so indebted to the club that he was preparing to join the club in sleeping rough for the night to promote the club's charity work:

> An Everton supporter is convinced that his beloved Blues saved his life. And 23-year-old Dylan Bannon will return to sleeping rough at Goodison Park tonight to highlight the support he received from Everton in the Community. Dylan, from Anfield, battled drug addiction and found himself sleeping rough just as the first national lockdown hit in 2020, plunging him further into his cocaine addiction and struggling to find a way out. He was put in touch with Everton's 'Home Is Where the Heart Is' programme in April 2020 and the charity supported Dylan with weekly check-ins over the phone and food vouchers, before referring him to a drug rehabilitation centre. Now, more than one year clean, he is determined to help others facing a similar experience and is championing the Goodison Sleepout to raise awareness of the charity's work. – David Prentice[29]

Another person that is regularly helped by the club at the highest level is Mark Cruise who suffers from motor neurone disease. In the Covid lockdown of 2020-21, he became the lockdown buddy of club manager Carlo Ancelotti who regularly phoned him during this period. During this lockdown period, the club also supported 27,000 families and made 25,000 check and welfare calls. It provided over 14,000 food parcels and over 250,000 meals for kids and the elderly. They even helped with energy bills and mobile phone credits for those living alone. These recent initiatives were a reaction by the club to the coronavirus crisis of 2020-21. They are bracketed under the title of the Blue Family Project.[30]

Perhaps, in the Premier League, the only club that comes close to Everton, in terms of its community involvement, is another one with a strongly local profile of support, Newcastle United. An independent Ernst & Young analysis in February 2019 showed that the club had contributed £236 million to the local economy in the 2017/18 season.

> The findings of the report were unveiled as the club took ownership of a Community Centre located just half a mile away from St. James' Park. The Project Pitch side initiative at Murray House intends to convert the venue into three floors buzzing with physical activity, for innovative classrooms, a 4G football pitch and a high-tech digital hub. The Centre is the latest venture undertaken by the Newcastle United Foundation, which invested £3.2m in projects across the North-East during season 2017/18. – Premier League[31]

In early 2020, the club responded to its reliance on a sport betting firm, SportPesa, as a shirt sponsor when it replaced them for one match with their own community programme on the shirts. The Everton chief executive, Denise Barrett-Baxendale, recognised at the club AGM that year '...that "in an ideal world" they would prefer a "different type of sponsor"...'[32] True to her word, later that year, the club not only changed their sponsor to the online car purchase company Cazoo, but, as part of the deal, they got Cazoo to donate up to £50,000 a year to Everton in the Community.[33]

It might also be said that SportPesa hadn't helped itself in 2017 by describing the club as a 'hopeless place' after posting a video of new manager Sam Allardyce dancing to the Rihanna song 'We Found Love'.

> SportPesa's tweet added: 'Sam Allardyce is set to become the new Everton manager! Talk about finding love in a hopeless place'. – Mark Critchley[34]

The club would seem to have been quick to end this deal, as the government are currently exploring a ban on shirt sponsorship by gambling companies, although this isn't expected to come into force before 2023. As of 2021, nine of the then Premier League teams and six Championship clubs were sponsored by betting companies.[35] The issue appears to be having increased relevance with events such as the screening of ex-Arsenal star Paul Merson's well-documented issues with gambling by the BBC on 11.10.2021 in the programme 'Paul Merson: Football, Gambling and Me'.

However, the club appeared to have blotted its ethical credentials in June 2022 when it announced a shirt sponsorship deal with online betting firm stake.com.

> Earlier this month, the Blues confirmed that they had agreed a club-record deal with Stake.com to replace Cazoo on the front of their shirts from the 2022/23 campaign onwards. The multi-year partnership is set to commence on July 1 and will also see the company's branding appear on screens and media backdrops at both Goodison Park and Finch Farm.

> However, the decision has divided supporters, who believe that Everton should not be in partnership with betting companies. A petition was set up shortly after the club's announcement calling for the decision to be reversed – and last week it reached over 20,000 signatures. – Adam Jones[36]

Another pioneering aspect of the club's community programme was the opening up of its free school in 2012. Everton was the first club in the country to do this. Yet another first from the programme is the planned 'People's Place', a building which will provide a dedicated space to expand on the club's mental health delivery and will promote positive mental and physical well-being. In February 2022, this scheme was awarded a substantial funding boost from the Premier League, the FA, and the government's Football Foundation.[37]

It is clear the Everton in the Community programme, particularly its local work, has cemented the club's roots in its local community. Despite its growing attempts to recreate itself as a global brand, this is unlikely to break the club's local bonds into the near future.

Despite the relative lack of success on the field in the Premiership era, Everton supporters have an incredibly strong identification with, and confidence in, the club. A recent survey showed that 95% of fans had confidence in the club, compared to a Premiership average of 77%. A staggering 92% said the club was well run, compared with a Premiership average of 78%.[38] In more recent years, this has barely diminished – at the end of season 2018/19 85.1% either strongly, or very strongly, agreed with the statement that 'Everton FC cares about its fans'. Given that the manager Marco Silva was to be sacked six months later, an astonishing 70% was satisfied with his performance.[39]

These figures are astonishing if compared to the club's recent lack of success on the pitch. It is also highly debatable if Everton's clear success in running its community programme is matched by its ability to manage its own finances. At the end of the 2019/20 season, the club had the least sustainable wages-to-revenue ratio in the entire English Premier League. It had a ratio of 84.9% compared with the best performance by Tottenham Hotspur of 38.8%.[40]

The figures obviously need to consider the club's antiquated ground and the relative lack of success on the pitch. However, these constraints didn't seem to restrain the club the following season when they 'splashed the cash' under new manager Carlo Ancelotti, including the £200,000 per week wages of Colombian superstar James Rodríguez. Yet, the following season, forced into relative austerity by the Financial Fair Play rules, the new boss Rafa Benítez has had to work with a very limited budget with their top signing Demarai Gray costing a mere £1.6 million. This book has been highly complimentary of the club's management over issues like fan engagement and its groundbreaking Everton in the Community scheme. However, its recent track record of appointing managers and relative profligacy on player spending, with no clear benefits on the pitch, leaves much to be desired. Periodically, the fans have rebelled against this apparent lack of achievement. In September 2015, shortly before the takeover of the club by Farhad Moshiri, a plane flew over Goodison Park organised by fans critical of Bill Kenwright's reign as Everton chairman. The banner it was pulling read: 'Your failures are your legacy.'[41]

A month earlier, there had been a protest meeting before the opening season match against Watford:

> ...at the back of the room there was a banner reading: 'Kenwright and Co, it's time to go – 20 years is plenty.' Yet their disaffection is about more than two decades without silverware. While the half-time boos at Goodison that afternoon had their root in two factors – frustration at the team's slow football and anxiety over a summer where Everton have, to this point, been the Premier League's lowest spenders – Sunday's protests reflect wider concerns.
> – Simon Hart[42]

More recently, towards the end of the humiliating 1-4 defeat at home to Liverpool after a seven-match run without a win, in December 2021, fans in the Gwladys Street end were heard to chant 'sack the board' on multiple occasions.[43] In the aftermath of the match, the club's director of football, Marcel Brands, resigned from the club after being berated by the fans at the end of the match. In the weeks preceding Rafa Benítez's sacking by the club in January 2022, there were numerous fan banners calling for the sacking of the board and protests outside the ground indicating growing disillusionment with the running of the club. In terms of the sacking of Benítez, the club did listen to the fans. However, at the time of writing, Kenwright and the rest of the board remain.

In spite of all this, the most recent Premier League National Fan Survey showed a staggering 94% of fans were impressed by Everton's conduct in response to coronavirus compared to a Premier League average of 73%. The fans were particularly impressed by the senior players and management team deferring their salaries for three months to enable all full and part-time employees to continue to be paid through the crisis, and also by the chairman and largest shareholder matching the £400,000 donated to the Blue Family project out of their own pockets. Perhaps the most revealing finding in the survey was that 84% believed the club listened to its supporters, 30% more than the Premier League average.[44]

A good illustration of how the club has listened to the voices of its supporters came in 2013 when the club tried to introduce a new club badge which would remove its traditional motto and wreaths. It would also remodel the character of Prince Rupert's Tower. After 22,000 fans signed a petition rejecting the change, the club suggested three possible new designs, all reflecting the fans' wishes. In the end, 78% supported the first suggestion which was eventually adopted.[45]

The intensely localised nature of Everton's support seems to be a big influence on this strong pattern of identity. A Premier League National Fan Survey from the mid 1990s indicated that Everton was the most locally supported club and Liverpool was the least locally supported.[46] The same survey showed that Everton had the highest proportion of fans that supported the club due to parental influence, 59%.[47] A more recent online survey found that 57.9% of participants lived in the north-west of England.[48]

The extent of Everton fans' identification with the city was amply illustrated in 2009 when, under intense pressure from the fan pressure group 'Keep Everton in our city', the club board dropped their proposal to move the ground out of the city to nearby Kirkby. This proposal came three years after the club failed to find the finances to fund the prestigious riverside stadium development at the King's Dock.

In December 2006, Everton joined the rush to move stadia to generate more income for over 20 years. The board announced the possibility of a move in conjunction with Knowsley Council and Tesco. The 50,000-seat stadium would be part of a £400 million development.

The club announced the move because – it would develop the brand; it would take advantage of multi-use facilities and a media-friendly stadium would be created. It must be said also that the stadium would have enormously expanded the club's income.

For Tesco, it would be able to construct a socially responsible corporate identity and help to build a brand community.

Showing a desire to consult the fans, and being aware of a growing opposition to the out-of-city stadium, Everton Chairman Bill Kenwright announced a ballot and the fans conducted a fierce debate and a grassroots organisation – 'Keep Everton in our city' – was formed which lobbied private and public institutions in the area and region.

In August 2008, the Secretary of State for Communities and Local Government ruled that the planning proposals breached local and regional planning policy and ordered a public inquiry.

In November 2009, he also agreed that the project breached local and regional area planning policy and would encourage business away from the town and city centre. After this, the proposal was dropped and the club committed itself to finding a new site in the city.[49]

Mindful of the failure of this proposal, the club has been careful to adopt a much more consultative approach to the more recent proposal to relocate the club's ground to the Bramley-Moore dockside site. Revealingly, the new stadium project was called 'The People's Project' by the club.

In October 2018, the club announced a two-stage public consultation process about moving to the new ground. The first three-week consultation started on 15th of November. This took the form of a series of exhibitions across Liverpool. The second stage would come in the summer of 2019 when the club would submit detailed plans including homes, health, and business facilities.[50] The Everton Chief Executive Denise Barrett-Baxendale said –

> Everton's chief executive Denise Barrett-Baxendale said: 'We would like as many people as possible – and not just football fans – to take part and let us know their views.' – Hamish Champ[51]

The club received 43,000 responses to the second-stage consultation which was believed to be the largest commercial undertaking in the city's history. It also had 20,000 responses to its first-stage consultation. The second-stage tour events were attended by 15,000 people including 2,726 non-Everton fans, 24% of whom had no interest in football. Overall, 98% of respondents supported the club's plans.[52]

The consultation process has been praised by independent outsiders such as Chris Daly, the head of the Chartered Institute of Marketing, who said:

> 'Strong brands put their customer at the heart of everything they do, and Everton's stadium consultation is a shining example of this. The club has not assumed, but asked fans what it is they want, inviting Evertonians and the wider public alike to play a meaningful part in the process,' stated Chris Daly, the head of CIM – Stephen Chapman[53]

The consultation process has also won awards. In November 2019, 'The People's Project' was awarded the Best Property and Construction Campaign at the Northern Marketing Awards.[54] In 2020, it was named winner in the 'Stakeholders in Planning' category at the national Planning Awards.[55]

'The People's Project' was unanimously supported by Liverpool Council's Planning Committee and was later approved at governmental level.

The undoubted success of the consultation process has underlined the club's particularly close relationship with its local community and cemented the local base of its traditional support.

By contrast, some other clubs have not developed similar consultative methods as Everton. Despite claiming to have consulted the fans about their move to the Olympic stadium in 2016, a survey of 2,431 West Ham fans by the Football Supporters' Association in 2012 found that nine out of ten opposed the move. Instead, it is claimed by the FSA that:

WHU'S VIEW? say: There has been no widespread consultation or attempt to seek the views of the vast majority of supporters. – Football Supporters Association[56]

In December 2019, Alan Kelly wrote an article explicitly advising Everton to avoid the mistakes made by West Ham in their stadium move. He was specifically concerned about in-ground issues such as attempts to sanitise the match atmosphere and a failure to specifically designate a home section in the stands. However, he did acknowledge that Everton did seem to have the fans in mind.[57]

Certainly, West Ham have been bedevilled by a series of fan protests since the move and, belatedly in 2020, they announced plans to build new stands closer to the pitch.

My own research, in my local Everton supporters' group in South West England, also supports the localism theory. Out of 25 supporters living in the West Country, 14 gave family reasons as the most important influence in supporting the club and 11 lived on Merseyside when they first decided to support Everton.[58]

This is further reinforced by a Premier League survey in 2007/08 which showed 54% citing parental influence as the main reason for attending their first match, the highest in the Premiership.[59]

Everton's local basis of support is also evident in its high levels of female and child support, as found by Jacqui McAssey in the independent fanzine *Girlfans*. She found that 20% of all active Everton fans were female – a higher than average proportion in the Premier League. She puts this down to the relative affordability of season tickets for both adults, juniors, and children – the latter season ticket was frozen again for the 2017/18 season at £95. She also found particularly high levels of family involvement attending matches including both male and female fans, from an early age.[60]

Everton's female fan base has also been encouraged by the club being an early pioneer of women's football. Everton Ladies, renamed Everton FC Women in 2019, was officially formed for the first time in 1995, although the club did have previous lives on the Wirral Peninsula as Hoylake WFC and later as Leasowe Pacific. In its first year in the then FA Women's Premier League, the only other current Premier League teams to be members of the league were Arsenal, Liverpool, and Wolverhampton Wanderers. In 2011, they were also one of eight inaugural members of the FA Women's Super League.

A lesser known, much earlier pioneering gesture was the match on Boxing Day 1920 when 53,000 crammed into Goodison Park – and a further 14,000 being locked outside – to watch a women's charity match between Dick, Kerr Ladies and St. Helens Ladies.[61]

Everton fans, possibly because of their localised support base, used to have a reputation for being particularly racist. As recently as 2000, a survey found that their fans had witnessed a higher percentage of racist abuse than any other British football club.[62] In the 1980s, their fans had even gained notoriety for throwing bananas at black Liverpool player John Barnes. However, in March 2004, the club were inducted into the 'Show Racism the Red Card' campaign in recognition of their hard work in trying to eliminate racism from the club. This work continues to the present day. This seems to have paid off because, in September 2019, fans in the Gwladys Street end launched a huge banner opposing the racist treatment in Italy that their Italian striker Moise Kean had experienced. A multicultural touch was evident with the Italian wording of 'No al Razzismo'.[63]

The club also has an LGBT+ group – the Rainbow Toffees – and in December 2018 it launched its 'Altogether Now Campaign' to celebrate the diversity and inclusivity of the club which in May 2020 it developed further by signing up as a Stonewall Diversity Champion.[64]

An interesting, and somewhat surprising, finding from a recent fan survey found that Everton supporters were the second most likely in the Premier League to have voted for Brexit.[65]

No less than 57% of Everton fans voted for Brexit, the only set of fans with a higher number were those of Chelsea with 61%. Paradoxically, Liverpool had the second highest remain vote with 77%.[66]

This finding is less surprising given that Merseyside generally voted Remain with 50.44% of the vote. But, significantly, for Everton fans, the two most working-class districts – St. Helens and Knowsley – voted Leave with 58% and 51.6% of the votes, respectively.[67]

Perhaps as a consequence of its local appeal, Everton fans continue to show exceptional levels of interest in, and identification with, their club. In 2002, a Premier League National Fan Survey indicated that Everton fans' devotion to the club was the highest in the Premier League with 37% answering yes to the question 'is football the most important thing in your life?', whereas Liverpool fans were second with positive response rates of 32%.[68] All this wealth of information confirms that Everton's core support's strong identity with the club is reinforced by both localism and social class. In 2019, Everton fans, who have a smaller fan base on You Tube, were shown to be the most likely in the Premier League to engage with club videos on YouTube. However, given the club's relative lack of global appeal, the same survey found that the club took a month to match Liverpool's daily growth on Facebook.[69] This finding is quite ironic in the context of Everton, in 2009, being the first Premier League club to set up a Facebook site.[70] Yet, should Everton ever become a major force in English football in the future, they could theoretically match the example of Manchester City, who accounted for half of the 12 million Premier League new Facebook fans in 2018. However, the wealth of Manchester City is allowing it to invest in Facebook as part of its global brand-building plans in a way that few other clubs can match.[71]

Even so, Everton has a large and growing overseas support, especially in Australia, the Republic of Ireland, South Africa, Thailand, and the United States of America. In 2002/03, Everton had a largely failed attempt to appeal to the Chinese market with their shirt sponsorship by the Chinese telecommunications company Kejian and the short-lived signings of Chinese internationals Li Tie and Li Weifeng. The more recent sponsorship of EFC by the Chang brewery was a more successful campaign which appeared to strengthen its support in Southeast Asia. The more recent acquisitions of Colombian players Yerry Mina and James Rodríguez also seem to have dramatically improved support in South America.

The club, under Carlo Ancelotti, were showing the potential to create a more globally supported base in the future. Indeed, the club showed a truly global reach in its recent marketing campaign with huge lights in Miami, New York's Times Square, and in Bogotá, Colombia's tallest tower advertising the signing of Colombia's biggest football star James Rodríguez.[72]

In March 2021, since the signing of Rodríguez, there had been a 6,000% increase in sales of Everton merchandise in Colombia since 2019. When Everton had their first win over Liverpool, at Anfield, for twenty-two years it drew in an audience of one million.[73]

In April 2021, the club announced the next stage of its international strategy with the appointment of Jurgen Mainka, a former CONCACAF chief commercial officer, as part of the strengthening of its international team in North America. The club announced a six-pillar strategy including: fan base growth, strategic partnership, brand and business development, the launch of an international academy, retail expansion, and international preseason tour plans. Although this all sounds a major departure from its traditional roots, Mainka emphasised that the strong familial bond with its supporters was a major selling point.[74]

A recent book by the legendary Dr. David France, compiler of the world's largest football memorabilia collection solely based on Everton FC, suggests that the club has a unique American heritage based on its early American tour in 1955:

> It was only ten years after the war, and everything was new and bright. The players went on the *Queen Elizabeth*. They had never flown before. They had never seen the cars and the neon-signs. It was eye-opening. – David France, Rob Sawyer and Darren Griffiths[75]

France also documents Everton's unique attraction to US fans in the book's survey:

> Everton is in a very poor part of Liverpool, a very poor part of the UK, and a very poor part of Europe, but Americans love history and Everton has an unparalleled history. One of the things about Everton is that it has never brought

shame on the city of its birth, and it has conducted itself in an appropriate way. – David France, Rob Sawyer and Darren Griffiths[76]

It seems that Everton's strong community values could paradoxically have an attraction to potential American fans that is more substantial than temporary success and a global image. These values are fully echoed by Cameron Jones of the Carolina Supporters' Club:

I can hold my head high and take pleasure in knowing I support a genuine football club driven by its community and supporters rather than simply by money. An example is the way Everton and its fans always stood by the side of their greatest rivals, Liverpool, during the darkest days of the Hillsborough tragedy. – Alex Dimond[77]

At the time of writing, Everton boasted 30 separate fan clubs in North America.[78] By basing its preseason tour in Florida in 2021, the club seemed intent on increasing these further.

In December 2021, the club also announced a new commercial partner in Asia to promote the growth of the club in that continent. In an apparent climbdown on their previous policy of dropping a betting firm as their shirt sponsor, they have signed a deal with the Asian betting firm i8.BET:

The deal will see i8.BET branding appear around Goodison Park, with the firm having access to player imagery for commercial purposes, while the betting company will use Everton's name and brand extensively across the region as part of its marketing strategy. – Dave Powell[79]

It has also become increasingly noticeable at home games to see growing numbers of foreign fans attending the match, even for a club with such a localised fan base as Everton.

This isn't surprising, as British tourism is increasingly dependent on foreign fans attending Premier League matches. In 2015, it was estimated that these fans brought in an overall economic gain to the country of £684 million, a 15% increase over 5 years.[80]

In 2018/19, slightly more than 800,000 foreign tourists went to a football match:

> ...almost one in every 43 visitors and over 40,000 international business visitors also managed to find time to go to a football match during their stay. With all of the sports Britain has to offer, it is the chance to experience a live football match which attracts the largest volume of inbound visitors. – Visit Britain.org[81]

The same survey showed that North West England is the top region for football tourism with 10.8% of the visits.[82]

All this must be taken into account when assessing the extent to which the club's support base remains localised. However, it still seems unlikely that it will become as globalised as the support base of Manchester United or Liverpool in the near future. This is especially the case in the USA where a recent fan poll of Premier League teams put Everton joint tenth on 1% support only above Bournemouth![83]

Overall, Everton fans, even in the age of a global Premiership, still have a remarkably local fan base. It remains one of the Premier League's best examples of a club that still puts the idea of community at the heart of its core philosophy. One of the main reasons for this is the evolution of the original fan base around the Stanley Park part of Liverpool. It must also be stated that Everton's relative lack of success in the Premiership era is another reason.

Since joining the Westcountry Blues supporters club in the late 1990s, I have been struck by the mix of people aboard the coach trips we regularly make from Taunton. As my research shows, almost half of the members appear to be exiled Scousers and their children. However, slightly over half are fans from the south-west of England which may indicate the way that Everton's localised support is gradually breaking down.[84] I could speculate that if, in future, the club has a similar run of success as it had in the 1980s, its localised support base could be totally transformed. In this era of globalisation, its worldwide support could be particularly transformed. This is one of the themes I will explore in the following chapter, to examine the extent to which Premier League fans, and particularly Everton fans, have been changed by developments in football since the 1960s.

4
CHANGES IN FOOTBALL
SINCE THE 1960S

Debates about religion and the traditional social background of a club's support became rapidly outdated after the formation of the English Premier League in 1992 and the subsequent formation of the UEFA Champions League in the same year. These competitions, with the associated massive influx of cash from satellite TV and associated spin-offs, have transformed not only the wealth of top-flight English teams but also the fan base of these clubs. The extent to which the all-seater, modern stadia of the Premier League, together with the globalisation and commercialisation of the game, have transformed the social basis of fans will be examined in this chapter. There will also be an examination of how the US franchise system of ownership of many Premier League clubs has impacted the fans.

It's too early to speculate on the consequences of multiple football clubs and other sporting club ownership, but it's unlikely to strengthen the bonds between the local community and club. It inevitably will enhance the global reach of these clubs, however, I will argue that these developments all have their genesis in the experiences of supporters attending games in the period from the 1960s till 1989 when the apparent glamorisation of the game, through TV coverage and the creation of media superstars like George Best, was in stark contrast to ordinary supporters attending run-down stadiums with the growing menace of hooliganism making football attendance an increasingly dangerous pastime.

There will be four distinct sections to the chapter – changes in the late twentieth century; changes in the twenty-first century; the evolution of a wider fan base; and the growing diversity of football fans.

There will be a particular focus on these developments for Everton fans. My own membership of Westcountry Blues based in South West England is a miniature consequence of these developments. The relative ease of transport, give or take the numerous hold-ups on the M5 and M6 due to accidents or roadworks, has enabled most members to be regular match attenders and season ticket holders. The club's presence on social media has also enabled members to follow the club daily, as many do throughout the world. The forces which created the club's localised fan base are rapidly changing and leading to a new type of fan.

The post-1960s developments of football could be said to be covered by two contemporary philosophical trends – globalisation and postmodernism.

According to Beck (2000), the process of globalisation brings about the greater significance of global spaces, events, problems, conflicts, and stories.[1] Its significance for this book will be examined through looking at the development of the Premier League with its growing global audience, the development of global ownership, together with relevant repercussions such as the attempted European Super League.

The term postmodernism developed in the post-war period as a rejection of the social identities forged by the Industrial Revolution and the development of the scientific era of the eighteenth to early twentieth centuries. You could argue that it was in this period that the traditional fan base of English football clubs was created. The theory was most famously developed by the French philosopher Jean-François Lyotard. He argued that the computer age would transform our knowledge base and enable us to increasingly create new identities.[2] This can be illustrated in football by the growing support of English Premier League clubs, not only in all regions of the UK but in all parts of the globe.

This idea will be developed in this book by looking at how social media and globalisation are transforming the identities of football fans. English football teams and their associated fan bases were essentially forged by the white, male working class in the late nineteenth and early twentieth centuries; they were essentially created by the Industrial Revolution. By the early twenty-first century, fans are becoming increasingly varied. Globally and nationally fans are increasingly picking and choosing their teams like you might choose between consumer products. We all know of 'glory hunters' who don't have firm support for a particular club but who temporarily choose clubs who are doing well. Arguably, this is a sign of how the top teams are ensuring a future support base that the others will find difficult to challenge. The consequences of this for supporters of Everton Football Club will be particularly emphasised.

> We no longer conform to the traditions of the old occupational cultures and instead we choose a lifestyle. This term, not in itself a new one, was taken by the advertising and designer culture of the 1980s to stand for the individuality the self-expression, that were the cornerstones of the free market revolution of that decade. The era of mass consumption, with its emphasis on conformity and similarity, has been replaced by an apparently endless choice and variety of consumer goods aimed at specific market segments. – Nigel Watson[3]

In terms of football, this process can be particularly seen with the spread of football to new markets in the Americas, Asia, and Africa. Increasingly, Premier League clubs are trying to appeal to these new markets, and in some cases, neglecting their core domestic support:

In truth, with globalisation and the lack of online borders, football clubs stopped being a portrayal of a local community. They now seem to be a representation of ideas and values that anyone can relate. Although the political trend within countries would suggest the opposite, when it comes to sports, globalisation has bulldozed walls, geographical boundaries, and prejudice, interconnecting institutions and people who share a sporting ideology. – Bruno Pantaleoni[4]

Football has been a global game since the early twentieth century after British sailors and industrialists had exported the game to the rest of Europe and South America. However, the game still was grounded in the traditions and values of the local area where it was played.

Over the decades, football became a global game, but one that reflected the local traditions of its fans. British fans sang during the games, inspired by working class songs and popular music. South American fans adopted a carnival style, using firecrackers to accompany the teams' matches. – Samuel Granados[5]

The social basis of British football fans has also been widened through the introduction of all-seater stadia. All-seater stadia, which were being phased in at the inception of the Premier League, were recommended prior to this by the 1989 Taylor Report in the wake of the Hillsborough tragedy of 15.04.1989 when 96 Liverpool fans were crushed to death at the FA Cup semi-final. There was also the wider background of the previous Ibrox tragedy in 1971 and the persistence of hooliganism culminating in the 1985 Heysel Stadium disaster.

The background to the Taylor Report was the post-war growth of match attendance. This was reflected at Everton FC with its record crowd being 78,299 in the Merseyside derby in November 1948. The club also briefly regained its status as having the highest average crowds in the seasons 1955/56, 1961/62, and the championship-winning season of 1962/63.[6]

However, the growth of crowds was not matched by any significant modernisation of the stadia. Football stadia historian Simon Inglis documents how from 1939 until 1971 very few changes were made to British football stadia:

> In fact, football grounds spent the next 30 years blissfully content with their pre-war designs, ideals, and standards. If not for the disaster at Bolton in 1946 there might have been even fewer changes than there were before the 1960s. Most of those that did occur were quantitative rather than qualitative, except at grounds recovering from war damage, or those of smaller clubs on the way up, such as Peterborough and Ipswich. – Simon Inglis[7]

The 1960s were, in retrospect, a golden era for Everton Football Club. As has been previously stated, it averaged the highest crowds in the 1962/63 season and in Ball, Harvey, and Kendall they were to have their greatest ever midfield which culminated in winning the 1969/70 Football League trophy.

England winning the World Cup in 1966, the abolition of the maximum footballer wage in 1961, and the consequent growth of celebrity footballers such as George Best gave football a new-found glamour which gave new supporters, such as me, an added attraction to the game.

> "In the 60s pop music came along, which had a big influence on what fans sung. They would sing Beatles songs on the terraces and gradually they kind of changed those songs and became more creative": Paul Brown, the author of 'Savage Enthusiasm: A History of Football Fans'. – Joel Sked[8]

The World Cup being staged in England in 1966 also gave fans a direct insight into the globalised world of football which the country had previously tended to ignore, not choosing to enter the World Cup until 1950, twenty years after its inception and not entering the new-found club European competitions in the late 1950s until pioneering managers like Matt Busby of Manchester United ignored the directive of the 'isolationist' Football League that had kept out previous season's champions Chelsea, and entered the European Cup in its second season of 1956. Ten years later, England hosted its first and, so far, only World Cup Finals. This competition had a particular resonance for me as a nine-year-old, as my club's Goodison Park would host reigning champions Brazil and matches up to the semi-final stage.

Unlike in London, local football fans entered the global spirit of the competition as a Swedish journalist reported:

"This is the football city of England – not stiff and serious London where you can hardly tell there is a World Cup competition going on," reported Swedish newspaper Dagens Nyheter in its coverage of games at Everton's Goodison Park stadium.

"I don't think I have ever heard a football crowd enjoy themselves as they did in last night's game between Brazil and Bulgaria," the paper's correspondent wrote.

There was something approaching a carnival atmosphere with the streets around the ground decorated with hanging baskets and bunting.

Kenny Leary, whose mother lived in Claudia Street, one of the terraced roads near the ground, said decorating it had been a tradition since VE Day.

"The streets around Goodison Park were all decorated and it became like the United Nations round there as fans from different countries came to look at the streets," he said. – BBC News[9]

There is also some evidence that the Brazilian team had a long-term impact on encouraging black fans to support football clubs in England.

It was less than two decades since the beginning of substantial migration from the Caribbean to the UK and migrants still faced exclusion from many sections of society, including football.

"To be honest we were cheering for Brazil, there weren't that many black role models in football so it had to be Brazil," said Wally Brown, an engineer who would later become a community leader in Toxteth.

He was also lucky enough to get a ticket for Portugal's famous 5-3 victory over North Korea in which Portugal's Eusebio, who was born in Mozambique, bagged four goals.

"The Portugal game was the first time I had been at the ground when there was a black player, it was an incredible atmosphere," added Mr Brown. – BBC News[10]

There was also a short-term boost to attendances but, due to the growth of hooliganism and the maintenance of antiquated grounds, this wasn't maintained into the following decades.

Attendances did receive a fillip from the World Cup victory and the following two seasons saw a rise to the 30 million mark, which represented the peak since the post-war heyday. – Richard Foster[11]

As a child in the 1960s, taken to the upper Gwladys Street Stand, I was sheltered to the potential hazards of standing on the terraces. However, the relative crush experienced in one brief stay in the now defunct boy's pen gave me an inkling. This was brought home to me in the early 1970s when large crowds often led to uncomfortable experiences of being forced against barriers in the paddock. Behind the goals, it was visible that the situation was even more uncomfortable. Goodison Park had previously experienced at least one example of crowd crushing in 1958 when, in a fourth round FA Cup match against Blackburn Rovers, two crash barriers broke and a hundred people were treated for injuries. Everton Football Club journalist James Cleary speculated that the official crowd of 75,818 was an underestimation of the 80,000 plus crowd that was widely speculated to be in the ground.[12] However, in the naïve days of the 1960s, we didn't think of the potential health and safety implications, but at some semi-conscious level they were felt. When the tragedies of Ibrox and Hillsborough occurred, I'm sure that I was among many thousands of fans who said to ourselves 'There but for the grace of God go I'.

Also, the seeds of hooliganism were also sown in this decade which were to have such a negative impact in the 1970s and '80s.

"Organised hooliganism started in the '60s and it really began on the football special trains being vandalised. There were more tribal elements to being a football fan. They were going to away [games] numbers in large numbers, very visible." ...

"By the 1970s most football grounds had been completely unchanged since they had been built in the Victorian era. They were desperate places, literally falling to bits. Fans were being treated as animals. That was another catalyst for the bubble which hooliganism flourished within": Paul

Brown, the author of 'Savage Enthusiasm: A History of Football Fans'. – Joel Sked[13]

In the 1960s, travelling to lesser home matches with my dad, I was totally oblivious to football hooliganism. However, when I had my season ticket in the early 1970s and was able to go to bigger matches, I gradually became aware of the threat. I first noticed it at the home game against Manchester United on the 23rd of February 1971. Toward the end of a hard-fought, 1-0 win, I noticed that the heart of the Gwladys Street terrace, home to the 'hardcore' fans, emptied ten minutes before the end of the game. What I didn't know, at the time, was that this 'hardcore' element rushed around both sides of the ground to ambush United fans coming out of the away stand and harass them all the two miles back to Lime Street station in the city centre. At my first away match the following month, the ill-fated FA Cup semi-final defeat to Liverpool at Old Trafford, Manchester, the United fans appeared to gain their revenge by sabotaging both sets of Merseyside fans after the match at Victoria station. Being relatively young and very naïve, I was terrified at the scenes which only lasted a few minutes before the United fans were dispersed by the police.

However, these incidents seemed very trivial after witnessing the horrific scenes in February 1973 when Everton were knocked out of the FA Cup at home to Second Division Millwall. Before the match, 11 Millwall fans entered the Gwladys Street end and charged at the Everton 'hard core'. The Everton fans regrouped and attacked with knives. I personally witnessed six Millwall fans being taken out of the ground on bloodstained stretchers. One of the fans had to be operated on later in Walton Hospital.[14]

This incident was the worst hooliganism I experienced. However, throughout the rest of the 1970s and into the 1980s, I frequently witnessed hooliganism, particularly at away games.

Hooliganism and the context of decaying Victorian grounds were the conditions which formed the background to the changes which were to transform football in the late twentieth century.

CHANGES IN THE LATE TWENTIETH CENTURY

Change was forced on the football authorities with a series of disasters that occurred in the late twentieth century beginning with the Ibrox disaster on 02.01.1971.

The tragedy occurred at the end of the traditional Hogmanay fixture between Glasgow Rangers and Glasgow Celtic. After Rangers scored a last-minute equaliser, 66 fans were crushed to death on stairway 13 as fans were leaving the massive home terraces. The Rangers ground had a history of safety issues.

The events of the 2nd of January 1971 are more correctly known as the Second Ibrox Disaster, as the ground had already tasted tragedy when a vast wooden terrace collapsed during a Scotland v England match in 1902, a disaster in its own right which killed twenty-five people.

In an ironic twist, what happened in 1902 actually led to the introduction of even more dangerous football stadia, as rotting wooden terraces were replaced by vast concrete stands capable of holding the weight of more people, but not necessarily able to cope with the consequences.

The huge rebuilding work that followed the first tragedy to occur at Ibrox meant that the home ground of Glasgow Rangers had become one of the three biggest grounds in Glasgow along with Celtic Park and Hampden Park. All three were seeing crowds of anything up to 100,000 at the time; but despite the stadiums growing rapidly there were few, if no, safety procedures in place to deal with the huge throngs that were now attending football matches week-after-week.

There was little regard for the safety and well-being of football fans back then – something which no doubt contributed to the death of two people in a crush at Ibrox, in September 1961 – a full 10 years before this mass loss of life on the very same spot. – Football Whispers[15]

Arising from the disaster, the government commissioned the Wheatley Report which eventually led to safety certificates being required by grounds for a capacity of over 10,000 under the Safety of Sports Grounds Act 1975. However, Rangers were determined to go one stage further and build a largely all-seater stadium.

Rangers rejected piecemeal development such as had plagued other grounds. They refused to compromise in size or materials. Ibrox was to have a new shape, three stands and, enough office and showroom space to create an income independent from football. And instead of luxury accommodation for a minority, Rangers opted for maximum comfort and an unimpeded view for all. – Simon Inglis[16]

They were able to spend the then staggering sum of £10 million over a three-year period because, at the time, they were richer than any other club due to their pools income. However, this income would be dwarfed by the commercial implications of future deals secured in England.

It is hard to examine what impact these changes have made on the traditional, Protestant, working-class fan base of Rangers. However, like most large British clubs, its fan base is changing. The all-seater atmosphere, together with the social changes of the last forty years, has led this once narrowly Protestant club to broaden out its target base. In 2019 it launched a new diversity and inclusion campaign, which hoped to show that Rangers was the place for you regardless of background, sexuality, faith, disability etc.[17]

The persistence of hooliganism in the English game through the 1980s and the series of tragedies culminating in Hillsborough in 1989 illustrated the shortcomings of the 1975 Safety of Sports Grounds Act and the failure of football to branch out from its traditional male, working-class support. It also saw average attendances plummeting to record post-war lows.

> The bleakest statistic in this slump in football's popularity was for the 1985-86 season, when the average gate for the entire Football League was 8,130 from an aggregate of 16,488,577. This compared with an average of 22,333 from an aggregate of 41,271,414 in 1948-49. – Jon Henderson[18]

Perhaps one of the events which directly led to the particularly low attendances of 1985/86 was the fire at Bradford City on 11.05.1985. A fire in the antiquated main stand with a wooden roof claimed the lives of 56 fans. Incredibly, the stand was due to be demolished two days later. The fire led to the Popplewell Inquiry which closed all wooden stands and banned their future building. Martin Fletcher, who had several relatives killed in the fire, was critical about both the club and the Popplewell final report.[19]

The year 1985 was to also coincide with the peak of post-war hooliganism in the English game. There were a series of incidents that included large-scale rioting at the match between Luton Town and Millwall on 13.03.1985. This led to the Thatcher government setting up a 'war cabinet' to tackle the problem.[20]

However, the most notorious incident involved Everton's arch-rivals Liverpool in the build-up to the European Cup Final of 1985 at the Heysel Stadium in Brussels.

Approximately an hour before the kick-off, Liverpool fans charged at a fence separating them from Juventus fans, a wall collapsed, and 39, mainly Italian fans, were killed.[21]

At the end of the month, the Thatcher government asked the FA to not enter English teams in European competitions. However, this was superseded a few days later when UEFA banned English clubs indefinitely. This was to have particularly devastating consequences for Everton Football Club when, arguably its greatest ever team, would be prevented from competing in the European Cup both for the following season and for 1987/88.

It is understandable that the preceding events continued to prevent the development of a broader fan base for football. A potentially more varied fan base was not going to be attracted to such a potentially dangerous and threatening atmosphere on ancient football terraces. *The Sunday Times* produced a lead editorial story at the time which seemed to sum up the state of the game:

A slum sport played in slum stadiums and increasingly watched by slum people, who deter decent folk from turning up. – *The Sunday Times*[22]

It was to take the biggest catastrophe of the lot to finally shake the football authorities out of their decades of complacency over the need to modernise stadia.

On 15th of April 1989, Liverpool were facing Nottingham Forest at Hillsborough. Coincidentally, I attended the other semi-final, Everton against Norwich City at Villa Park at the same time on that day. I was so shocked by the Hillsborough tragedy that I gave up my ticket to the subsequent Liverpool v Everton FA Cup Final.

Due to the South Yorkshire police's desire to prevent mixing of the fans, Liverpool, the much bigger club, were allocated the smaller Leppings Lane end of the ground which was situated to the west and consequently nearer to Liverpool. It must be said that the background of hooliganism, which played no part on the day, strongly influenced the circumstances to the tragedy. This was for two reasons: firstly, most top-flight clubs had built steel fencing separating terrace fans from the pitch; and secondly, the police decided to house the fans in totally inappropriate ends of the ground and forced the Liverpool fans to access the Leppings Lane end, and the side North Stand, through one entrance. The Leppings Lane end had also incorporated five pens, ironically enough to prevent sideways crushing. With ten minutes until kick-off and an estimated 5,000 more fans trying to get in, the police ordered that two extra gates and an exit gate be opened. The great majority of these fans entered two of the central pens which were already overcrowded with spectators. There was no effective stewarding to usher the remaining fans into the less crowded, outer pens. In the resulting crush, 96 fans died. As football ground historian Simon Inglis has indicated, the tragedy was entirely preventable:

Despite having a larger fanbase, Liverpool, to their annoyance were, as in 1988, allocated the smaller Leppings Lane End of Hillsborough, consisting of a seated tier accessed from one block of turnstiles, and a terrace for 10,100 standing spectators, accessed by just seven turnstiles.

Even by the standards of the day this was inadequate and resulted in more than 5,000 Liverpool supporters pressing outside as the 3pm kick-off approached. Had the start of the match been delayed, the crush may well have been managed. Instead, the South Yorkshire Police's Match Commander, David Duckenfield, ordered one of the exit gates to be opened, allowing 2,000 fans to rush through.

Those who turned right or left towards the corner pens found room. However, most headed unwittingly, with no warnings from stewards or the police, to the already packed central pen, accessed via a 23m-long tunnel.

As the tunnel filled, those at the front of the terrace found themselves pressed up against steel mesh perimeter fences, erected in 1977 as an anti-hooligan measure. Incredibly, with fans patently suffering within full view of the police (who had a control room overlooking the terrace), the match kicked off and continued for nearly six minutes until a halt was called. – Simon Inglis[23]

The tragedy directly led to the Thatcher government commissioning the Taylor Report whose recommendations on football ground safety were to transform not just the game but, I would also argue, its fan base. In particular, the development of all-seater stadia would create the conditions to attract a more female and diverse fan base. Not only were these stadia more comfortable, but they also minimised further developments of hooliganism, at least inside the grounds.

But the Taylor Report was not solely responsible for these changes. Many commentators see the formation of the English Premier League, in 1992, as a direct consequence of the decline of the game in the 1980s.[24] Aided by the growing revenues from Sky TV, it was the vehicle that was to transform both English football and its consequently changing fan base.

In the 1980s, some of the top clubs threatened to break away from the Football League. In 1986, they succeeded in raising the First Division share of revenue to 50%. They also demanded that TV companies pay more.[25]

The success of this move, together with the financial consequences of the ban on English teams from European competitions, gave the impetus for the foundation of the

Premier League in 1992. It was also the case that the financial implications of the Taylor Report recommendations were crucial to the final announcement of the breakaway from the Football League and the search to maximise revenue. The top clubs were struggling to finance the requirements for all-seater stadia and welcomed the opportunity to significantly increase their revenues.[26]

Greg Dyke, the chief executive of London Weekend TV and chairman of ITV Sport played a crucial role in encouraging the clubs to break away, although his London Weekend Television package would eventually be outbid by Rupert Murdoch's BSkyB package.

The other crucial player was David Dein, deputy chairman of Arsenal.

Dein was fascinated by the high-rolling razzmatazz of American sport and frustrated by the endless sub-committees of the Football League, the competition to which his club then belonged. – Paul MacInnes[27]

Both men were initially trying to get the then big five clubs: Liverpool, Arsenal, Tottenham Hotspur, Manchester United, and Everton to negotiate their own TV deal, separate to the Football League. Another key player was future Liverpool chief executive officer and the first chief executive of the Premier League, Rick Parry. In 1992, encouraged by the FA, Parry chaired a meeting of the then First Division clubs at which the basic rules of the new Premier League, including the crucial decision not to redistribute a share of TV money to lower league teams, were finalised.

In that meeting, which lasted less than two hours, the clubs and Parry created the founders' agreement. It is not legally-binding, but it has acquired a kind of sanctity, close to that of a religious text. Inside were two simple changes that were to prove incredibly profound. The first was that, within the Premier League, everything would be voted on by the clubs, every club would have one vote, and every vote would require a two-thirds majority to pass. There would be no committees or sub-committees. Secondly, at the behest of the smaller clubs, all TV revenue would be split in a new way. The Premier League would no longer share its money with the lower divisions. But neither would the Big Five take a share commensurate to their size. All money would be divided 50-25-25. 50% was to be split equally between the clubs, 25% according to the league position achieved in the previous season and only 25% dependent on the number of times a club appeared on TV. (A footnote: any international TV revenues, which then were nigh-on zero, were to be divided equally.) – Paul MacInnes[28]

These rules would ensure that the eventual winner in the bidding for the new Premier League would be Sky, as clubs outside the big five had resented the previous attempt by ITV to negotiate a separate deal with the big five.[29]

Sky would be the Premier League's first television partner. Their bid worth £44.5 million a year outstripped ITV's, by £12.5 million a year; plus, they had promised to show more matches and devote greater time to the broadcasts, transforming live football into a genuine television product. – Joshua Robinson and Jonathan Clegg[30]

Over the years, Sky's financial commitment to the Premiership would rocket to £760 million in 2012. When they were joined by BT Sport in 2016, the two businesses combined to pay £4.2 billion for a three-year deal. Even the BBC committed £204 million for its highlights package.[31]

In June 2018, Amazon Prime entered the frame with another £90 million for its three-year deal Christmas festival package.[32]

The English Premier League is now so popular globally that in 2021 it was transmitted to 190 UN member states. This is how the League projects itself globally:

The Premier League worked in conjunction with its international broadcast partners throughout Season 2020/21 to develop innovative ways of engaging supporters around the world.

Former Premier League players Michael Owen and Richard Dunne were the stars of a pre-match show for Chinese partner Tencent ahead of the fixture between Manchester City and Leeds United in April 2021, interacting live with Tencent's studio guests in Beijing as well as answering questions submitted by fans.

In India, Star Sports was involved in bespoke programming tied to the 2021 Next Gen event, which underlined the Premier League and Indian Super League's (ISL) continued commitment to developing football in the country.

Newcastle United icons Alan Shearer and Steven Taylor took part in a special show which was produced by PLP for broadcast across Star Sports' network the day before the ISL final.

The show offered a new opportunity for ISL fans to engage with the Premier League, as the former Magpies players selected some of their favourite moments of the season.

The Premier League's ambassador for India, Ranveer Singh, was the face of Star Sports' 'Sunday Night Football' campaign, promoting some of the biggest Premier League fixtures of the season which took place in prime viewing slots on Sunday evening in the country.

While fans in Asia watch Premier League matches at night-time, US-based supporters often get up in the early hours to tune in to live fixtures broadcast by NBC Sports.

To thank dedicated fans for their commitment, the Premier League distributed an exclusive 'Breakfast in Bed' kit including a Premier League-branded dressing gown, breakfast tray and mug so they could enjoy a #MyPLMorning breakfast while watching matches.

In November, 1,000 lucky Stateside fans were served up tasty Thanksgiving treats as a show of gratitude for their support. – Premier League[33]

The other major cash injection into the pockets of the top European clubs was the formation of the UEFA Champions League also in 1992. Like the English Premier League, the impetus for its formation was a threatened breakaway by the top European clubs led by Silvio Berlusconi's AC Milan.

Regular format changes have been introduced to maximise revenue for the top clubs.

The introduction of a group stage and multiple competitors from the same nation increased match numbers, as well as the number of renowned clubs involved. The end result was financially rewarding, with more high-level clashes increasing interest and earnings across the planet. – Christopher Atkins[34]

The changes have also worked to benefit clubs from the top five European countries that bring in the most TV revenue. Stefan Szymanski, writing in 2007, records that:

In 1993 the desire to create more games among the best teams led to the creation of the European Champions League (to replace the knock-out format that had hitherto existed). Since most of the money generated by this competition came from TV contracts in the big five countries, clubs from these countries lobbied for a larger share of the rents, and in 1997 UEFA granted these countries up to 4 places in the tournament, in contrast to the single place they had formerly received. As a result, big clubs in big countries saw a significant boost to their income, while clubs from smaller countries found it harder to compete. For example, in the three decades between 1967 and 1996 43% of [the] semi-final places in the top European club competition were taken by teams from the big 5 countries, while in the last decade they have taken 90% of the places. This has little to do with the increasing strength of their squads, and much to do with their share of places in the competition increasing from 13% at the beginning of the 1990s to nearly 50% by 200. – Stefan Szymanski[35]

By 2015, the global audience for the Champions League final was dwarfing that of the US Super League Grand Final:

Despite record breaking numbers in 2015, the Super Bowl is in fact not the biggest sporting event of the year. The UEFA Champions League Final, which takes place on Saturday in Berlin, puts the popular American event to shame when it comes to viewership.

In addition to an impressive 200 countries tuning in, the teams in this year's finals made off with $108 million in prize money, dwarfing the Super Bowl's $14.9 million collected during the playoffs in January.

The UEFA Champions League last year drew a global audience of 380 million viewers, while Super Bowl XLIX had the attention of 114 million viewers, a record for US television. The Super Bowl has an international audience, but the numbers are too small to make a significant difference. – Max Kraidelman[36]

The revenue generated by the Champions League has greatly increased. Between 2003/4 and 2018/19 broadcasting revenue quintupled from 450 million euros to 2.40 billion euros.[37]

CHANGES IN THE TWENTY-FIRST CENTURY

One of the consequences of the increased revenue, which has also come from increasingly lucrative TV deals to cover the Premier League, is to attract a new pattern of ownership, particularly foreign ownership. By 2013, half of the clubs in the Premier League and Championship had foreign owners. The results of this have been mixed. Certainly, for Chelsea and Manchester City the new owners have pumped millions of pounds into their clubs which have enabled them to become two of the top clubs in the world. However, for many of the other clubs the consequences have often been negative and include:

...buying a club purely to make a profit; lack of financial transparency; poor communications and relationships with staff and fans; ignorance of history and tradition (e. g. the decision of Cardiff City's Malaysian owners to push through a change in club colours from traditional blue to 'lucky' red); and possible vested interest in such matters as playing games abroad and watering down promotion and relegation. – Steve Tongue[38]

This is another article to foresee events of eight years later with the proposed European Super League.

This new pattern of ownership has also enabled some clubs to take over other foreign teams with a view of using them as potential feeders and therefore extending their club's global appeal. Not surprisingly, even after Abu Dhabi has invested £2.5 million in the club itself, Manchester City have a controlling interest in more foreign clubs than any other club in the world; overall, five men's teams, two women's, and a minority stake in another. Their stated intention is to have a club in every continent with 'City' in their name.

> The City Football Group are without doubt the most significant multi-club owners in world football right now, themselves a subsidiary of Sheikh Mansour owned private equity company Abu Dhabi United Group. ...

> Manchester City are, of course, CFG's primary asset, but they acquired Manchester City Women and 80% of New York City FC in 2012, followed by Melbourne City in 2014 and both Club Atletico Torque and Girona in 2017. – Alfie Potts Harmer[39]

A further 19 English clubs, ten of which are in the current Premier League, have at least one foreign club as a feeder club. This means that half of the current Premier League have foreign feeder clubs. Everton don't appear on this list. [40]

Another consequence of foreign ownership of clubs is the crossover between Premier League club ownership and other sporting club ownership, particularly when it is linked to American sporting clubs. One must bear in mind that previously we have mentioned the attraction of the American sports model for David Dein in instigating the Premier League.

In early 2021, Jack Kiely listed six out of 20 Premier League club owners who were also owners, or part owners, of American sporting teams.[41]

Two of the most prominent of these owners are John W. Henry of the Fenway Sports Group, joint owners of Liverpool Football Club and the Boston Red Sox baseball club, and Stan Kroenke, joint owner of Arsenal FC and the NFL side the LA Rams.

Although the Fenway group have broadly been popular with the fans, they have taken three key decisions, based on the American sporting model, which were not only unpopular, but fan power forced the club owners into embarrassing U-turns. Firstly, in 2006, they attempted to charge the fans the highest priced ticket in the Premier League, £77 to sit in the main stand. They also reduced the number of hospitality packages for ordinary fans and increased their price. This led to 10,000 fans walking out of the Sunderland match in 2016 and the ticket prices being frozen to the present day. Then in 2020, during the Covid pandemic, the club tried to put various non-playing staff on a government-funded job retention scheme, despite the club making a £42 million profit. After various ex-players and fans protested, the plan was abandoned. The final U-turn, the eventual withdrawal from the European Super League, will be discussed later in this chapter.[42]

Rather more successful at cutting 55 jobs at his Premier League club in 2021 was Arsenal owner Stan Kroenke. As well as owning the NFL side the LA Rams, he also owns the American basketball team the Denver Nuggets, the ice hockey team the Colorado Avalanche, and the American soccer team the Colorado Rapids. His unpopularity with Arsenal fans is well documented, for example in 2019:

...Gunners fans issued a joint statement calling on him to reinvigorate the club.

The statement said supporters had 'never felt more marginalised'. The club then sacked Unai Emery and hired Mikel Arteta. – Will Pugh[43]

In England, the major impact of this money is to greatly widen the wealth gap between those of the top five or six clubs and the rest. The huge impact of player wages to its majority foreign workforce is the most obvious product of all this spending to the general public. However, the focus of this book is on the fans, so the effects of this money on the fans will be tackled next.

THE EVOLUTION OF A WIDER FAN BASE

One of the most immediately pressing issues for fans is the increased price of match tickets. In 2014, it was estimated that, if Manchester United had increased its cheapest tickets from 1989/90 in line with inflation, its tickets would have risen from £3.50 to £6.94. Its actual cheapest ticket was £31. This represented a 785% increase from 1990 to 2014 in the club's cheapest tickets. In the first few years of the Premier League, Manchester United season tickets increased by 70% over a four-year period.[44] Over the same time span, Liverpool's cheapest tickets had increased 1,150%. Even so, both clubs were charging less than the top London clubs. In that same season, Arsenal's cheapest season ticket broke the £1,000 barrier. It is worth noting that predominantly fan-owned German champions Bayern Munich's standing season tickets were £114.00.[45]

In 2018, a report found that British fans spend more on football than anywhere else in Europe.

> British football fans spend on average £712 each year on football through a combination of watching games on TV, travelling to matches and buying merchandise. The hardcore Premier League fan spends a whopping £1,118 ...

By complete contrast, German fans are spending half as much as English fans on average (£353), helped in part thanks to considerably lower ticket prices. – fcbusiness[46]

It is worth noting at this point that Everton's ticketing policies stand in marked contrast to most of its Premier League rivals which is one of the many reasons for the greater fan support of the club's management. At the start of the 2020/21 season, it announced the fifth consecutive year that season ticket prices had remained the same. The club is particularly keen to nurture its young support, with particularly low prices for the under 18-year-olds, meaning that one in six season ticket holders are under the age of 18 compared with a Premier League average of one in eight.[47]

An independent ranking of all Premier League clubs classified Everton as having the third cheapest season tickets, ahead of Burnley and Sheffield United, at the start of the 2019/20 season.[48]

The increase in ticket prices and the creation of modern stadia is transforming the social base of Premier League fans. In 2018, Dr. Michael Skey summarised this change:

'So the traditional working class people that used to watch football are being priced out and what we're seeing is more affluent middle-class people entering the game, becoming interested in the game,' Skey said. 'And there is a huge debate at the moment in the UK about what's called "plastic fans." These are fans who do not seem to be authentic. They do not seem to be linked to a particular club; they simply follow them because they're successful.'
– Michael Skey[49]

The Manchester United fan Professor Geoff Pearson described how the social mix of fans on the once fanatical Stretford End has changed in the era of the Premier League:

"It's a very different make-up of fan on the Stretford End," he says. "You've got fans there now who are tourists. And there are people who have been completely priced out of the game. Rather than go to every match, they'll go two or three times a season.

"There are more families now; more people who are tourists, who might go to one game at United one day and then plan a trip to Chelsea or Arsenal the next week. That's had an impact on how the stadiums feel."

The perception now is that football grounds at the highest level have grown sterile, a narrative endorsed by those tourist fans holding camera phones aloft and the multiplying of half-and-half scarves sold by vendors outside. – Philip Buckingham[50]

Perhaps the ultimate illustration of the changing identity of football fans was an article in 2019 on NBC Sports news which invited US fans to choose an English Premier League team to support and, helpfully, included a guide for each team to aid US consumers in making their choice. This was the section on Everton:

Everton gives you the ability to back a team with proud history, and a team involved in one of the best rivalries in sports (The Merseyside Derby with Liverpool). The team has not been afraid to spend to bring exciting talent like Gylfi Sigurdsson and Richarlison, and also possesses one of the heroes of England's World Cup run in goalkeeper Jordan Pickford. The additions of Yerry Mina from Barcelona and loanee Kurt Zouma from Chelsea mean the Toffees may be primed to surge high up the table, and the club is one that prides itself on its status in the community, too. A lot to like here. – Nicholas Mendola[51]

On a similar theme, the American website 32 Flags gave five reasons for supporting Liverpool FC:

1. The Fans – The greatest asset to LFC is its fans. Widely considered one of the more knowledgeable fanbases, they try to take their club anthem, "You'll Never Walk Alone", to heart.

2. Young Team – This squad has the youngest age average (25.6) of the entire EPL and, while it shows negatively sometimes, it definitely leads to an optimistic outlook for many who feel the future is bright.

3. Exciting play – Last season, Liverpool were the most exciting team to watch. While this wasn't great for fans' hearts, a leaky defense never is, the swashbuckling offense the team displayed was awe-inspiring.

4. Club History – The second most successful club in England, second only to Manchester United, this club has a unique history filled with great players, and great managers. Do yourself a favor and look up Bill Shankly.

5. Team on the Up – Even though this season has been a disappointment, many will agree that this team, with its young squad, young manager, and forward thinking philosophy, the trend is upward. – Jeff Snyder[52]

The same identity conundrum was given a British twist in 2021 by the exiled Scottish journalist Jon Davey when he used Benedict Anderson's idea of an 'imagined community' to explain how Scots can decide whether to support the England football team or not, which English team to support, and to share a new affinity with fans previously not identified with.

Like many Scottish football fans, I have an English team. Sharing much of our media with our neighbours south of the border, it is easy to follow the fortunes of English clubs. – Jon Davey[53]

He goes on to explain how he has chosen to support the England team in 2021 under Gareth Southgate after years of supporting England opponents:

> ...as England manager he made a break with the past. He challenged the football orthodoxies, brought in new players and new ways of doing things and played down the jingoism and the expectation. His pre-tournament message seemed well thought out and covered much more than football. – Jon Davey[54]

Another consequence of the rise in global communications is the rise of 'dual fandom'. Living in South West England, I must confess that my second club is Yeovil Town FC. However, it hasn't affected my main footballing identity remaining with Everton. The phrase 'dual fandom' has been coined by Dóczi and Tóth in a survey of football supporters living in Plymouth in 2007.

> In the world of globalized football, it has become a tendency that fans follow the results of competitions in other countries, and therefore, they might become enthusiastic supporters of a foreign club. This is especially so in countries with less remarkable achievements and a lower standard of competitive football, where football enthusiasts become (less traditionally but more rationally) attached to teams from the most televised leagues. In case of English interviewees, the real essence of dual fandom can be grasped especially when an English fan really supports two teams, two English teams. An illustrative description of dual fandom can be found in the following quote:

> 'Supporting a local team is a kind of local identity, it represents your roots, it's your heritage. The fact that you were born in Plymouth and the team is called Plymouth

is a close association, although the feeling is essentially primitive, tribal and native. The support of a team like Liverpool comes from the desire to want to be connected to success.' (Supporter of Plymouth Argyle and Liverpool FC, aged 51) – Tamás Dóczi and András Kálmán Tóth[55]

This dual identity is well illustrated by the nineteenth-century sociologist Ferdinand Tönnies in his concepts of Gemeinschaft and Gesellschaft. Gemeinschaft can be literally translated as meaning the word community as associated with premodern societies. In a football sense, this could be linked to feelings of family and neighbourhood which the Plymouth supporter above describes as 'primitive, tribal and native'. It illustrates the community origins of all our football clubs. Gesellschaft, however, shows how relationships change in modern industrial societies to people being more individualistic with self-interest and the pursuit of money binding people together. Again, the above supporter shows this in his support of Liverpool and him wanting a connection with success.[56] The idea of choosing a team to reflect changing identities, on a national and global scale, can also be related to this concept. It can also be related to the increasing monetary connections between people. In the English Premier League rising ticket prices seem to be creating a new type of fan.

Perhaps the most visible signs of these changes can be seen among London clubs whose match tickets have increased the most. In 2018, this is what a casual attender at Arsenal's Emirates Stadium observed:

Originally, Arsenal fans were mainly working-class, but it was apparent at the match we attended that it was the liberal elite's favourite club. Back when the club was at the Highbury stadium, matches were filled with working-class characteristics: affordable tickets, poor but full stadium and hooliganism. Since it moved to the glamorous

60,000-capacity Emirates stadium, working-class fans were driven out by expensive seasonal tickets. (Saraswati)[57]

It was observable that a lot of the fans were from the middle class. Despite the high ticket price per person, many people came with their entire family. Moreover, a sizeable number of ticketholders were children under 16, reflecting that their families' financial resources allowed them this indulgence. The crowd did not exactly look classy, but formal items like suits and laptop bags of people who came straight from work were easily noticed. There were also different areas of seating, divided by view and price (the two went together) and it seemed like the people with more money would sit on the high-rise balconies with full view of the stadium. – Sociology in London[58]

Another club in London that has been accused of alienating its traditional male, working-class base is West Ham United who, in 2016, moved to the London Stadium that hosted the 2012 London Olympics and was legally required to keep its athletics track keeping fans at a significant distance from the pitch. This has led to fan protests and trouble inside the ground over issues like segregation and the ban on fans standing.[59]

The soaring increase in football revenues has also attracted a different type of owner who are willing to change the whole commercial structure of clubs:

A pay-per-view model and more televised games attracted bigger investors willing to buy players with soaring salaries to ensure wins on the pitch. In the beginning club members were the owners of their teams, their stadiums and training facilities. But as business featured larger and larger in the sport, this model changed. Stadiums were named for companies and players wore advertisements on their shirts. – Samuel Granados[60]

One of the other consequences of the money flowing into the Premier League is the influx of foreign ownership, which has further widened the fan base by using their control to broaden their clubs' global appeal. In April 2020, only seven of the 20 Premier League clubs were not predominantly foreign owned and one of those seven, Newcastle United, seemed on the brink of foreign ownership.[61]

The latter became a reality in October 2021 when a Saudi-based consortium controversially took control of the club. The deal appears to have gone through as a result of the new owners guaranteeing that they weren't controlled by the Saudi state. Many commentators believe that the consequences for the club could be as significant as the foreign takeovers of Chelsea and Manchester City. With an initial takeover value of £300 million, the football finance expert Kieran Maguire estimated that, due to previous owner Mike Ashley's frugality, the club could have £205 million to spend in the next transfer market which could totally transform the prospects of the club.[62]

The club's local face of the Saudi consortium, local businesswoman Amanda Staveley, stated after the takeover:

'Our ambition is aligned with the fans – to create a consistently successful team that's regularly competing for major trophies and generates pride across the globe.'
– Louise Taylor[63]

When asked if winning the Premier League title was the long-term aim she said:

'Absolutely ... Newcastle United is the best team in the world. We want to see it get those trophies, obviously. At top of the Premier League, in Europe, but to get trophies means patience, investment, time.' – Louise Taylor[64]

However, at the time of writing, there is some doubt about how long and whether Newcastle United can use their potential riches to become a top club.

Newcastle United's controversial £305m takeover by a Saudi Arabian-backed consortium has made them one of the richest clubs in the world – but the club will still need a "revolution" to succeed.

That's according to former Manchester City technical director Mike Rigg, who was tasked with transforming the squad when City's 2008 takeover was completed by their Abu Dhabi owners. – Alistair Magowan[65]

He lists six steps that the club needs to take if it's to challenge the elite, including:

'Create a new mindset...'; 'Walk away from 'pay day' players...'; 'Owners need to trust people to do their jobs'; [and] 'Prepare for bumps in the road'. – Alistair Magowan[66]

Perhaps the club most transformed by foreign ownership is Manchester City whose 2008 takeover, by one of the world's richest men, the Abu Dhabi Sheikh Mansour, has totally transformed the club and its traditionally localised fan base. He injected over one billion pounds of funding, transforming their team from perennial failures to arguably the world's best team in 2021. In 2018, Kevin Parker, the general secretary of the official supporters' club, described how the club had gone global:

'We probably had 80 branches and half a dozen internationally ten years ago,' he explained. 'Now we have 250 worldwide and almost 50 per cent are now international: in America, Indonesia, Vietnam, Singapore, China; there are two in Costa Rica.

'The difference is when we used to open branches they were ex-pats who'd travelled the world and settled down and still loved City to let everyone know in that part of the world.

'Generally that's not the case now, they're all locals. This is the wonder of the internet and media that people pick up on little bits and pieces and getting hooked.

'I went to New York for the City game [against Liverpool in July]. We'd flown 11 hours and there were people who had driven for 8,9,10,11, 12 hours to get to the game from all parts of the US and Canada. They were as dyed-in-the-wool Blue as I was and there's an element of me that's not comfortable saying that.' – Simon Bajkowski[67]

Everton, whose major shareholder is the Iranian Farhad Moshiri, owning 77.2% of the shares, are no different from this trend. However, the consequences for fan alienation seemed markedly different, and Moshiri is known to spend significant sums on the many charitable projects involved in the Everton in the Community programme.[68]

One of the first major foreign takeovers of a Premier League club was that of the American Glazer family over Manchester United in 2005. There had already been failed previous attempts to buy the Premier League's biggest, and potentially, most profitable club. The most notorious of these was the failed bid by Rupert Murdoch in 1998. This was met by large amounts of fan resistance including some supporter groups set against the takeover which was eventually blocked by the Labour government due to it being opposed by the Monopolies and Mergers Commission.[69]

The supporters' group was led by the well-known Channel 4 journalist Michael Crick, and they used novel tactics like writing to all 30,000 small shareholders to attend the AGM which was secretly filmed and sent to the media. The success of 'fan power' in this instance was to inspire opposition to the proposed European Super League in 2021. However, the group was eventually unable to prevent the next takeover of the club.[70]

In 2005, the club was taken over by the American Glazer family. They were undoubtedly attracted to the growing profitability of the club – the ex-chairman Martin Edwards has documented how, when he first had a stake in the club in 1980, it was valued at £32 million and when he sold his stake in 2003 it was £3 billion. This price dramatically increased after the Champions League victory in 1999.[71]

There was a determined campaign to oppose the takeover including the famous wearing of yellow and green colours on match days, the original colours of the club. There were also protests outside the ground, including burning effigies of the club's new owners. The protests grew after the Glazers loaded a previously profitable club with £717 million worth of debt. However, with the success of the club on the field, it won the Champions League five times between 2007-2013, the protests died down.[72]

One of the fan groups opposing the Murdoch takeover went into hibernation for several years only to re-emerge in 2005 to oppose the Glazer takeover. It had only temporarily abandoned their 'last resort' idea of setting up a separate club which was later to be known as FC United of Manchester. As well as opposing the Glazer takeover, they were also reacting against many of the changes to the fan experience which would be echoed at all other Premier League clubs: changing kick-off times to fit in with TV schedules, soulless, all-seater stadia, heavy-handed stewarding, and inflated ticket prices.[73]

Today, FC United of Manchester is the largest fan-owned club in the country and has tried to live up to the people's club image of the original Manchester United formed by the railway workers of Newton Heath. One of its many policies to discourage fan alienation is the ban on shirt sponsorship. [74]

Having built its own new stadium in 2015, there was a deliberate attempt to flee from the expensive, all-seater, and increasingly passive Premier League fan experience by creating a terrace behind one of the goals. The club was formed as a community benefit society with 4,200 paying members. In 2014, its community work served 2,000 people with a particular emphasis on helping struggling young people in one of Manchester's most deprived districts.[75]

Perhaps the most famous foreign takeover of a Premier League club was that of Chelsea in 2003 by the Russian oil and gas oligarch Roman Abramovich. Due to the club's subsequent success and the fact that he rescued a club with £23 million of debt, he has remained popular with the fans. One of the factors that clearly differs with Everton is the global reach of the club. This is closely linked with the Abramovich takeover which has dramatically extended the club's appeal in countries like USA, Korea, and China.[76] Abramovich has also endeared himself to the fans during the Covid pandemic by not furloughing any of the club's staff.[77]

However, the sacking of Frank Lampard in January 2021 did lead to fan protests carrying banners such as 'In Frank We Trust' appearing outside the ground. Also, the appointment of Thomas Tuchel on only an eighteen-month contract does perhaps show how dependant Abramovich is on continuing success to remain popular with the fans.[78]

Also, the continuing strength of fan power at Chelsea would be seen in the crucial role that Chelsea fans played in bringing an end to the proposed European Super League in April 2021.

More and more, top Premiership clubs are courting an increasingly global fan base which could come at the cost of their traditional local one.

The concept of a football match and its crowd being the optimal way for interested parties to watch a game is now only part of the contemporary football experience.

A football stadium, in most cases, can only host around 40,000 people, so there is a limit to how many people can gain access to the live event in person. However, the onset of global TV audiences has resulted in the most valuable football brands in the world [having] internalised this and expanded to markets overseas in order to generate higher revenues from regional corporate sponsors and engage with newer fans. With the onset of COVID-19 and the possibility of matches being played behind closed doors, the value of fans outside of a club's immediate domicile is more important than ever.

Clubs are entities that appeal to football followers globally. Whilst this appeal has been well documented in mature markets such as Europe, there is a growing base of more affluent fans in the likes of Asia and the Americas. At this precise moment, small children in the streets of Marrakech or Mumbai are walking around with a Manchester United, Real Madrid or Juventus replica shirt on their back. Football, because of its simplicity, is a universal currency that breaks down barriers, brings common interest to the table, and – above all – provides stimulation.

Football's natural audience has changed and has long since moved from the old working-class stereotype, dominated by men. There are new fans in younger populations, and crowds of tomorrow are far more tech-savvy, and extremely mobile. How else can supporters in China, India, and South America connect with a club in the north of England without harnessing the technological tools at their disposal? – Declan Ahern[79]

Global pressures on English football will surely increase further after the announcement in November 2021 of a new deal to sell Premier League matches to the USA for a record £1.1 million. This marks a 50% rise over a six-year period.

This brings the overseas TV income up to £4 billion which should rise further after 2022.[80]

Not surprisingly this deal will benefit the top Premier League clubs the most. From 2022, half of the total of overseas rights is now distributed according to where a club finishes in the Premier League. This will mean that the champions are set to get an extra £25 million a season going down to the bottom club getting an extra £9 million. The big clubs had their way after arguing that it was them who are attracting the extra TV viewers.[81] All of these developments have encouraged the growing diversification of football fans.

THE GROWING DIVERSITY OF FOOTBALL FANS

In the twenty-first century, there has been a growing percentage of female football fans. In 2019, it was estimated that the percentage of female fans in the English Premiership had grown from 25% in the 2014/15 season to 30% four seasons later.[82]

During recent years, Premier League clubs have also encouraged more female fans through a variety of initiatives. Perhaps the most visible is the creation of women's teams. Starting in season 1991/92 they, together with the Football Association, helped found the FA Women's Premier League national division. In 2010, this became the FA Women's Super League. In 2014, a second division was created and in 2018 the Women's Super League became fully professional. These developments are part of a global trend which today makes women's football the fastest-growing sport in the world.

In the past decade things have really gone from strength to strength as more and more elite clubs take on women's squads on a full-time basis, and grassroots outfits try to ensure that as many girls teams as possible thrive where practicable.

It's not an exaggeration to say that you'd be hard-pressed to find a competitive girls or ladies league even as recently as 2010.

However, the game continues to rise and remains the fastest growing sport in the world. – WGP Global[83]

These developments are in stark contrast to the initial FA reaction toward the early playing of the game by women. On Boxing Day 1920, 53,000 spectators crammed into Everton's Goodison Park to watch Dick, Kerr Ladies play St. Helens. However, the match gained notoriety for the wrong reasons when the match led to a whole series of restrictions on women's football culminating with the women's game being banned by a unanimous vote of the FA in December 1921. The FA cited strong opinions against the suitability of football as a reason for the banning of such matches. This ban stood until 1969. However, the women's game didn't vanish during this period. The major female teams were forced into touring the world during the domestic ban. For example, Manchester Corinthians raised money for charity through their world tours and, together with the Nomads, they had raised more than £275,000 for the International Red Cross by 1969.[84]

The FA saw the ladies' game as a threat to the men's game which was just being reorganised after the disruptions caused by World War 1. They cited the lack of match funds going to charity and used various spurious medical reasons for the ban:

'Complaints have also been made as to the conditions under which some of these matches have been arranged and played, and the appropriation of receipts to other than charitable objects.

'The Council are further of the opinion that an excessive proportion of the receipts are absorbed in expenses and an inadequate percentage devoted to charitable objects.

'For these reasons the Council request clubs belonging to the association to refuse the use of their grounds for such matches'.

Among the opinions from the medical profession who came out in support of the FA, Dr Elizabeth Sloan Chesser said: 'There are physical reasons why the game is harmful to women. It's a rough game at any time, but it is much more harmful to women than men. They may receive injuries from which they may never recover'.

Doctor Mary Scharlieb, a Harley Street Physician said, 'I consider football a most unsuitable game, too much for a womans frame'.

Mr Eustace Miles said, 'I consider football quite an inappropriate game for most women, especially if they haven't been medically tested first'.

Naturally, the girls were devastated and thought that the FA had taken this decision because they were drawing bigger crowds than some of the mens games, they thought they were jealous. It was perfectly acceptable for the female frame to do any manual task to keep the country going during the War, but to suggest that playing football could affect their fertility and that they were actually too delicate to play, was nothing less than insulting. – dickkerrladies.com[85]

Over these years, there has been a significant increase in finance for the women's game. In 2019, the league was sponsored by Barclays bank who put £20 million into the game. In 2021, there was a big breakthrough with the announcement that BBC and Sky were to put £24 million into the game over a three-year period with over 50 games to be broadcast live on TV.[86]

This deal has the potential to transform the women's game in England:

> For football supporters, the true maker of the success of this deal will show itself on the football field. This investment into women's football in England, particularly grassroots football should lead to success on a wider, global scale. At the club level, Women's Super league sides have been a step behind European giants such as Wolfsburg, Barcelona, and Lyon. If a WSL side were to win the Women's Champions League in the next few years, that would mark the triumph of this backing. This applies to an even greater degree if the national team has success on the international stage, having reached the semi-finals of the 2017 Euro's and 2019 World Cup. – Damola Odeyemi[87]

An important aspect of the deal is the involvement of the BBC which will be airing 22 WSL games and the Women's FA Cup. This is part of a strategy by the WSL to find a new audience for the sport.

However, the big clubs haven't always invested so heavily, with the country's biggest club Manchester United notably absent from women's football until 2018. This led to the club being heavily criticised by USA star Megan Rapinoe:

> 'It's 2020. How long has the Premier League been around? And we're only just seeing a club like Manchester United put effort and pounds towards a women's team? Frankly, it's disgraceful.' – Goal[88]

But the Premier League and Football Association have been encouraging the development of the women's game for a while. In 2013, the Premier League launched its 'Premier League Girls Football' campaign. The campaign had two aims – to increase the number of women and girls playing football and to develop their skills, confidence, and progress within the game. By 2016/17, 88 professional clubs and almost 23,000 girls and women had taken part.[89]

Another development to encourage female fans has been the provision of free sanitary products. In 2018, Brighton became the first Premier League cub to provide this service with Liverpool and Everton also discussing the same initiative:

> The On the Ball campaign was launched in Scotland by students Orlaith Duffy, Erin Slaven and Mikaela McKinley in an effort to increase the visibility of female football fans. But it has now spread across the UK with 13 clubs, including Barnsley in League One, signed up to the initiative. McKinley said: 'I think it takes us back to the role football clubs have a part in the community beyond football. A lot of smaller clubs were quick to come on board because they're perhaps a bit more in tune with what their fan base wants. But in terms of visibility it's great to have a Premier League club on board.' – Martha Kelner[90]

Many clubs now have their own women's supporter groups including Watford whose group, Women of Watford FC, was set up by fan Kate Lewers in 2021. She was inspired both by asking to speak by the club on International Women's Day and the killing of Sarah Everard by an off-duty police officer in March of that year.

> The aims of WOW are very simple: to give women more of a voice within the club, to encourage and promote a more diverse fanbase, and to inspire and empower future generations of female fans. – Watford FC Staff[91]

On the evening of 03.03.2021, Marketing Executive Sarah Everard was walking home in Clapham, South London, when she was abducted and murdered by the off-duty Metropolitan Police officer Wayne Couzens.[92] In the light of the murder of Sarah Everard, one of the aims of the Watford group was to create safe spaces for female fans, particularly when attending away matches.[93]

Another area of growing diversity among Premier League supporters is ethnic minority fans. A Populus poll in 2008/09 found that 8% of fans were from ethnic minority backgrounds with 16% among those fans who had only being attending for the last five years.[94]

These figures mark a significant increase since the 1960s and seventies. This rise seems to coincide with the increased profile enjoyed by the 'Kick It Out' organisation:

Working throughout the football, educational and community sectors to challenge discrimination, encourage inclusive practices and campaign for positive change, Kick It Out is at the heart of the fight against discrimination for everyone who plays, watches or works in football.

A small independent charity, the 'Let's Kick Racism Out of Football' campaign was established in 1993 in response to widespread calls from clubs, players and fans to tackle racist attitudes existing within the game. Kick It Out was then established as a body in 1997 as it widened out its objectives to cover all aspects of discrimination, inequality and exclusion. – www.kickitout.org[95]

In June 2020, the FA announced their support for the 'Black Lives Matter' campaign:

In an unprecedented move, Premier League players from all 20 clubs united in solidarity with this message and the Premier League supported their request to replace their names on the back of playing shirts with 'Black Lives Matter' and then display the Black Lives Matter logo on their match shirts.

We're proud to support the Black Lives Matter message in order to show solidarity to the Black community and to highlight inequality and injustice experienced by this community.

As an apolitical organisation and, while we are pleased to offer our solidarity in promoting this important message, we do not endorse any political organisation or movement, nor support any group that calls for violence or condones illegal activity.

We'll continue to stand firm against all types of discrimination. Just as we specifically promote campaigns like Rainbow Laces to support the LGBTQ community or Level Playing Field's week of action to highlight discrimination against disabled people, we are supporting Black Lives Matter.

To support the message, a Black Lives Matter logo has appeared on shirts in both the Premier League and Emirates FA Cup, along with a badge thanking the NHS for their work during the COVID-19 crisis. In addition, we will continue to support players who "take a knee" before or during matches. – www.thefa.com[96]

At the time of writing, the controversial 'taking the knee' was still being performed by a majority of Premier League players before every match.

The campaign was given a major boost in February 2021 when the English Premier League announced its 'No Room for Racism' campaign.[97]

However, 'Kick It Out' is still having increased cases of racism reported to it as it announced in 2019:

In November Kick It Out, football's anti-discrimination organisation, reported an 11% rise in reports of discriminatory abuse last season. The organisation received 520 complaints through its anonymised reporting system, with racism up by 22% and homophobia by 9%, and it is likely the figures will rise again this year. Worryingly the statistics do not take into account unreported allegations of abuse, raising the possibility that the situation is worse than Kick It Out's figures suggest. – Jacob Steinberg[98]

Another area of broadening support has been in growing efforts to attract the backing of the LGBT community. In 1989, the Gay Football Supporters' Network was formed which went on to promote the view that homosexuality did not preclude an active interest in and support for the game. It has a national network split into regions where Football fans of different ages and genders meet regularly to discuss their favourite sport and chat. Each co-ordinator submits a monthly report on activities and social events, and these reports are then included in the network's monthly newsletter which is posted to members.

They are also actively involved in campaigning on football-related issues. As well as providing a forum for gay football supporters to meet, the GFSN also campaigns against anti-homosexual discrimination in support of the FA's 'Football For All' programme. The FA encourages all clubs to endorse a gay-tolerant position, paralleling similar calls in the 1980s for clubs to support racial tolerance.[99]

They have had a major impact on many English clubs, noticeably at Arsenal. Arsenal's broadened appeal to the LGBT community was noted by *The Times* columnist Helen Rumbelow, in December 2021, after watching an Arsenal match for the first time in 30 years having been put off from watching a match in south London due to 'a few hours of being crushed by gangs of testosterone-poisoned punchy people'. She became reconnected to the game after noticing the club consciously broadening its appeal:

> Sure, there still weren't that many more women, but there was a noticeable change in sexual politics. The stadium displayed a huge Gay Gooners banner, and at half-time they interviewed one of the Gay Gooners' organisers who explained that in 2013 they became the first LGBT+ football-supporters group in England and have since grown to be the world's biggest. – Helen Rumbelow[100]

In 2017, 30 of England's 92 league clubs had LGBT fans' groups.[101] In 2013, the gay rights group Stonewall initiated a campaign to distribute rainbow laces to all professional footballers in the UK to promote the awareness of gay rights in football:

> In September 2013 Paddy Power, in association with leading gay rights charity Stonewall, set out to tackle homophobia in football by distributing rainbow-coloured football laces (Rainbow Laces) to every professional player in the UK.
>
> Why? Society and other sports have moved on. But there are more than 5,000 professional footballers across England, Scotland and Wales and none of them feels comfortable enough to come out as being openly gay. – Paddy Power[102]

This campaign had by 2021 over a million people wearing the laces in sport.[103] It has subsequently won official backing from the Premier League.

However, there are still numerous examples of homophobia among football fans as this survey from 2017 indicates:

43% of LGBTQ+ people think public sporting events aren't a welcoming space for them. (YouGov for Stonewall, 2017). – Rainbow Laces, Stonewall[104]

Another increasing element in football is the growing consumption of the game through social media. The top clubs are increasingly facilitating this. At Manchester City, the club have provided a high-speed wireless system at the Etihad Arena to enable fans to share their experiences on social media during games.[105]

Another method is through making branded content:

This can involve making a promotional video, Facebook Lives or something like a 'behind the scenes' from an event. Content like this makes a football fans feel like they are really part of the club they support. – Frankie Weaver[106]

For example, Norwich City put a video on YouTube in the build-up to their derby with Ipswich Town in 2018. Chelsea engages its supporters worldwide with a match day Twitter feed constantly updating fans by providing information about every part of the club.[107]

Dr. Alex Fenton has shown how social media benefits not only clubs, but also fans and players through messages, discussions, and interactions.

It also allows them to reach a wider audience than just local people and that could be national or international. It also gives a voice to fans, which can be a positive or negative thing. The Black Lives Matter campaign was active through players and clubs unfolded a range of opinions played out on social media. Meanwhile, female fans can be underrepresented on open social media channels and turn to closed or hidden online communities. – Alex Fenton[108]

Having said this, there is also clearly a negative side to social media with both fans and players being victims of online abuse and bullying. This came to a climax in April 2021 with players and clubs uniting in a four-day boycott of social media. This followed a series of high-profile racist abuse cases involving Liverpool players after the club's defeat by Real Madrid in early April and the Aston Villa defender Tyrone Mings revealing Instagram racist abuse.[109]

The effect of the campaign arguably was limited in view of the events three months later when three black England players were subjected to online abuse after missing penalties at the end of the Euro 2020 final.

Perhaps the ultimate consequence of the commercialisation and globalisation of football happened in April 2021 when six Premiership clubs and three each from Italy and Spain announced the creation of a proposed European Super League that would guarantee permanent membership for the original signed up members. These plans, influenced by the growth of US club owners, particularly in the Premier League, wanted to replicate the US Franchise System where clubs are protected from promotion and relegation and owners make money by cornering the market.

The plans entirely omitted to consult the views of fans, which was a fatal mistake, as events were to prove. It is worth stating that social media played a vital part in the fan campaign against this proposed league.

The plan was given immediate impetus by the financial losses incurred by the big clubs, particularly Real Madrid and Barcelona, during the global Covid crisis. However, the long-term cause was undoubtedly the growth of global, particularly American, ownership of the top European teams, and the European Super League revealed that the plan was for it to shadow the teams. In fact, the blueprint for the league was almost exclusively based on the US sports league model:

Leaked documents for the European Super League revealed that the plan was for it to closely shadow the structure of leading US sports leagues amid claims that games could be less than 90 minutes.

The Times has been told that similar to the American football, and basketball leagues, the proposals included plans to cap clubs' salary payments and clubs would earn huge profits from revenue-sharing agreements.

The cap on player salaries was to be 55 per cent of club income. European clubs typically spend about 70-80 per cent on salaries.

The 'closed' structure of the league also resembled American sports where teams are not relegated if they perform poorly – guaranteeing them a lucrative source of income.

Of the 12 European teams that signed up for the league this week, four have American owners: Manchester United, Liverpool, Arsenal and AC Milan. – Ben Ellery, Callum Jones, and Steven Swinford[110]

It was a sign of Everton's relative decline over a thirty-year period that, unlike in 1992 when it was one of the top five founders of the Premier League, it was excluded from these plans. However, the club's particularly critical reaction against the proposals, and the example of it being excluded, were key factors in the collapse of the scheme. It is particularly revealing that the club put the interest of the fans first in opposing the proposals:

Everton is saddened and disappointed to see proposals of a breakaway league pushed forward by six clubs. Six clubs acting entirely in their own interests. Six clubs tarnishing the reputation of our league and the game. Six clubs choosing to disrespect every other club with whom they sit around the Premier League table. Six clubs taking for granted and even betraying the majority of football supporters across our country and beyond. At this time of national and international crisis – and a defining period for our game – clubs should be working together collaboratively with the ideals of our game and its supporters uppermost. – Everton Football Club[111]

The Barcelona and Spain player Gerard Piqué even mentioned the example of Everton in his opposition to the plans:

'Do we want this for football? That Seville, Valencia, Everton, Leicester, Naples disappear?' – Phil Kirkbride[112]

The plans for the European Super League lasted a mere 72 hours. The strength of fan opposition from the six English clubs involved was critical to the collapse.

In the statements that signalled their departure, the six Premier League clubs were keen to assert that their decision was a result of them 'listening to supporters'.

While the truth of the matter is far more complex, it is obvious that fan protests did play a role. Right from the outset supporters have made their feelings clear. Liverpool and Leeds came together before their meeting on Monday night, while [there] were also protests outside the stadiums of Manchester United, Manchester City, Arsenal and Tottenham.

Seemingly the most effective demonstration of all was held by Chelsea supporters prior to their 0-0 draw at home to Brighton last night. Over 1,000 of the Stamford

Bridge faithful turned up with big bags of cans and banners, singing anti-Super League chants and preventing the team bus from entering the ground, leading almost directly to the news that the club was pulling out. – Matt O'Connor-Simpson[113]

However, the most visible illustration of fan power throughout this crisis was the resurfacing of the opposition to the Glazers' control of Manchester United on Sunday the first of May 2021 when fans, protesting outside Old Trafford, managed to break into the ground and prevented the playing of the Manchester United versus Liverpool game. There were also protests outside the other participating clubs' stadia. A particularly important one was that of Chelsea fans protesting before the game against Brighton the previous Monday.

The forced postponement of the Manchester United – Liverpool game was the ultimate proof of the continuity of fan power.

David Webber, course leader in Football Studies at Southampton's Solent University, told Al Jazeera that it was a 'tipping point'.

'This degree of direct action has changed the parameters of the politically possible. By disrupting and potentially cancelling one of the biggest games in world football, these distinctly local protests have gone global. They remind us how important – even in an age of global investors, and global fan bases – these local fans and these local spaces are.' – James Brownsell[114]

It's very clear that the US franchise system was key to the plans. Writing ten years before the ESL plans first were announced, Rupert Cornwell wrote a remarkably accurate article appearing to forecast future events:

American owners make money by cornering the market. In France, Italy, and even England, teams can rise from nowhere. ... Its major sports – gridiron football, basketball, hockey and baseball – all operate closed leagues. The same teams (either 30 or 32 of them, depending on the league) play each other, year in, year out. Only if their owners so decide is their number increased, in a process called 'expansion', dictated not by the excellence of a new team, but the potential of a new market. – Rupert Cornwell[115]

There seemed to be a miscalculation made by the owners, particularly the American ones, in the degree of fan loyalty and motivation for supporting clubs. Stacey Pope, associate professor in the Department of Sport and Exercise Sciences at Durham University, told Al Jazeera:

'Therefore, football is not like other activities. Normally, if you're not happy with the service when you purchase something, you would think about going with a different product or brand next time around. But being a football fan means you stick with a club through thick and thin, ie: you just don't change your membership or season ticket and switch to another team. Football has always been a game for the fans; it is 'their' club. But the current model of club ownership and running clubs as businesses suggests the reality is very different.' – James Brownsell[116]

There is also some evidence that it isn't just the older and more working-class fans who have rejected the ESL, but also many of the younger and even global fans. Owen Laverty, chief information officer at 'Ear to the Ground', a global sports agency, found this in compiling a fan intelligence agency called 'The New Breed of Fan' in 2021:

'Off the back of the European Super League, many people assumed it was only the traditional fans who rebelled against the concept,' adds Laverty. 'And fans in global markets, or younger fans, loved the idea. All of our research showed this wasn't the case.

'This is a fundamental part of the new breed of football fan. They are seeking the game of football to innovate and improve but that doesn't mean they will jump on any shiny new approach with lots of money behind it. They disliked the European Super League because it wasn't done for the betterment of football.' – Philip Buckingham[117]

However, it was not just fan power that destroyed the proposals. *The Guardian* has emphasised the role of the Football Association:

The Football Association had taken a key stand earlier on Tuesday when it warned that any club involved would be banned from the Premier League and all domestic competitions. – David Hytner, Andy Hunter, and Jamie Jackson[118]

The FA was also given important support by the UK government:

The FA's chief executive, Mark Bullingham, emboldened by the UK government's pledge to do whatever it took in legislative terms to block the breakaway tournament, said his organisation would take an uncompromising line with the rebel clubs.

Bullingham articulated the FA's stance in a meeting with Premier League officials, including the chief executive, Richard Masters, and the division's other 14 clubs, who were united in their opposition to the big six's scheme. – David Hytner, Andy Hunter, and Jamie Jackson[119]

So clearly other bodies were involved in the rapid disintegration of the plans, but the role of the fans was crucial. A prime example of this was in the belated apology to Liverpool fans by its American owner J. W. Henry, one of the main instigators of the ESL levy on top-flight transfers to support lower league teams.

The government's promise of future legislation appeared to be a step nearer in November 2021 with the publication of the Crouch report. This report has promised to protect the interests of the fans over owners in the wake of the demise of the European Super League. It has been inspired not just by this but also the Saudi takeover of Newcastle United and the financial worries of lower league teams such as Bury who were wound up in 2019. Its main proposal is to set up an independent regulator to protect the interests of the fans. It seems significant for this book that on the 11-member review panel that compiled the report, the only representative of the Premier League was Denise Barrett-Baxendale, the chief executive of Everton FC.

The 162-page report written by Tracey Crouch MP with the assistance of an expert panel, calls for the formation of an independent regulator for English football with powers that would extend to seizing control of a club from their owner. Today the government will give its public support to the formation of a regulator, which would also introduce a single owners' and directors' test that would have placed the controversial takeover of Newcastle United by Saudi Arabia's sovereign wealth fund under far greater scrutiny. – Matt Lawton[120]

The rapid collapse of the European Super League proposals and the setting up of the Crouch report indicated the continuing power of supporters, despite the growth of global finance in apparently controlling football. These developments have also given hope to the future of a club like Everton who have invested so much in their local community and have retained a particularly close link with its supporters. They have also kept up to date with changes in the game like being an early club to set up a women's team and, more recently, encouraging a global fan base. It also has a pioneering community programme.

The extent to which a fan base of Everton's size can remain localised, as it traditionally has been, is debatable considering all the developments that have been outlined in this chapter. However, the club's local community work and the continued relative lack of success of the club would indicate, that in the short term at least, the club's predominantly localised fan base is unlikely to change.

CONCLUSION

The early history of Everton Football Club, based in both religious communities and firmly grounded in the poorer wards of North Liverpool, has created a very socially similar and loyal fan base. Everton fans to this day are particularly loyal and mainly locally based in an era of globally based English Premiership club supporters. In 2013, Manchester United were estimated to have a global fan base of 355 million, Chelsea had 135 million, Arsenal had 113 million, and Liverpool had 18 million.[1]

There are no reliable figures for Everton FC, but its fan base is clearly much below the previously mentioned teams. Developments in post-war football have affected the club, but they are yet to acquire the wider and more diverse fan bases that the top five or six Premier League clubs have achieved since the modernising changes brought about through the creation of the English Premier League in 1992. However, it must be recognised that Everton fans are also growing globally with concentrations in the USA and Southeast Asia, the former mainly founded by expats and the latter through their long-term sponsorship by the Thai brewers 'Chang'.[2]

The club's official American fan club 'Everton in the USA' claims over 60 regional clubs and members in every city and state.[3] The Chicago Everton supporters' club celebrated its twentieth anniversary in 2021. This club eventually formed 'Everton USA'[4]

The ownership of the club by Farhad Moshiri has certainly encouraged these developments. It also waits to be seen what impact the building of a state-of-the-art stadium at

Bramley-Moore Dock will have on the traditional, localised, working-class fan base. Certainly, some of the accompanying planning would seem to be encouraging a more affluent and global fan base:

> Liverpool Council's planning committee gave unanimous approval to the proposals for a 'boutique hotel' metres from the stadium site this morning.
>
> The plans, from ZWY Lettings, will see the vacant warehouse at 66 Regent Road converted and brought back into use.
>
> It is likely to be one of many developments around the stadium, which will draw tens of thousands of people on match days to an area that currently sees few visitors.
>
> Everton's proposals for a new stadium cleared their final hurdle at the end of last week after the government confirmed they would not call the plans in for further consideration.
>
> That means Liverpool Council's earlier decision to approve the stadium design, which was also unanimous, stands.
>
> A report previously submitted to councillors said the entirety of the building would be utilised by the hotel, with its height also being increased.
>
> The report said: 'The proposal is for the conversion of a vacant warehouse into a boutique hotel. The proposal also includes increasing the height of the property to provide a further floor of accommodation.
>
> 'The site is constrained on all sides but will provide 65.5m2 of usable accommodation on each floor plus a further 65.5m2 in the basement.

'The proposed hotel would offer 9no. bedrooms with ground floor reception and general storage, together with provision for recycling, refuse and secure cycle storage. The basement area will provide food preparation and dining space.'

As well as potential new developments around Bramley-Moore Dock, there will also be improvements to existing facilities. – Nick Tyrrell[5]

Despite these developments, Everton's core support remains concentrated in and around the city of Liverpool, with concentrations in North Liverpool. The extent to which this will remain the case, ironically, depends on the club maintaining its relative lack of success. As the example of Manchester United shows, a traditional, locally based club has the potential to become a global phenomenon.

Manchester United have been named as the world's most popular club in new figures released.

Research from global market research agency, Kantar, shows United have a worldwide fan and follower base of 1.1 billion, an increase of over 400 million since a similar survey was conducted in 2012.

The survey, which was conducted across 39 countries and included over 54,000 respondents, showed that United's total amount of fans and followers has increased from 659m seven years ago.

United's latest figure have seen steady increases across Europe, Middle East and Africa, and the Americas, while the largest increases was in the Asia Pacific region, particularly in China, where the number of fans and followers grew from 108 million in 2012 to 253 million. – Richard Fey[6]

For now, Everton seem unlikely to replicate this any time soon. However, this was seen to be the case with Manchester United at the start of the 1960s!

Everton Fans – References

Introduction

1. Neville Southall – *Howard's Way* Sky Documentaries 2021

2. ToffeeWeb – History – Everton Average Attendances

3. Chris Beesley – 'How Everton became "The People's Club" – David Moyes lifts the lid on iconic moment' 18.03.19 *Liverpool Echo*

4. Who are the Orangemen?' 11.07.12 BBC News

Chapter 1

1. James Walvin – *The People's Game The Social History of British Football* 1975 Allen Lane

2. James Walvin, op. cit.

3. Second Reform Act 1867 – www.parliament.uk

4. David Kennedy and Michael Collins – 'Community Politics in Liverpool and the Governance of professional football in the late nineteenth century' *The Historical Journal* 2006 Cambridge University Press

5. Tony Mason – 'The Blues and the Reds – A History of the Liverpool and Everton football clubs' 1985 The History Society of Lancashire and Cheshire

6. Peter Lupson – *Thank God for Football!* 2006 Azure

7. Muscular Christianity' – infed.org

8. David Kennedy – *A Social and Political History of Liverpool and Everton Football Clubs: The Split* 1878-1914 2017 Routledge

9. David Kennedy, op. cit.

10. Peter Lupson – *Thank God for Football!* 2006 Azure

11. David and Peter Kennedy – *Irish Football Clubs in Liverpool* 2017 Amazon

12. David and Peter Kennedy, op. cit.

13. Peter Lupson – *Thank God for Football!* 2006 Azure

14. Peter Lupson, op. cit.

15. Thomas Keates *History of the Everton Football Club 1878-1928* 1998 Desert Island Books

16. Peter Lupson – *Thank God for Football!* 2006 Azure

17. Peter Lupson – *Thank God for Football!* 2006 Azure

18. Peter Lupson, op. cit.

19. GotfriedFuchs.blogspot.com – 'Bootle v Everton – The Original Merseyside Derby' 27.10.13

20. Derek Hodgson – *The Everton Story* 1979 Arthur Barker Ltd

21. Thomas Keates – *History of the Everton Football Club 1878-1928* 1998 Desert Island Books

22. Thomas Keates, op. cit.

23. Interview with Iain Mackie, Football Development Officer for Lancashire F.A. 25.01.22

24. Thomas Keates, op. cit.

25. Peter Lupson – *Thank God for Football!* 2006 Azure

26. Stevesfootballstats.uk – 'The Football League'

27. Thomas Keates, op. cit.

28. Thomas John Preston – 'The origins and development of Association Football in the Liverpool district, c. 1879 until c.1915' 2007 University of Central Lancashire

29. Thomas Keates – *History of the Everton Football Club 1878-1928* 1998 Desert Island Books

30. David Kennedy and Michael Collins – 'Community Politics in Liverpool and the Governance of professional football in the late nineteenth century' *The Historical Journal* 2006 Cambridge University Press

31. James Walvin, op. cit.

32. James Corbett – *Everton the School of Science* 2004 Pan MacMillan

33. James Corbett, op. cit.

34. GottfriedFuchs.blogspot.com – 'Bootle v Everton – The Original Merseyside Derby' 27.10.13

35. David Kennedy – *A Social and Political History of Liverpool and Everton Football Clubs: The Split 1878-1914* 2017 Routledge

36. Mark Metcalf – *Everton FC 1890-91: The First Kings of Anfield* 2013 Amberley Publishing Ltd

37. James Walvin – *The People's Game The Social History of British Football* 1975 Allen Lane

38. Thomas Keates, op. cit.

39. Re-election (Football League) – Wikipedia

40. https://en.wikipedia.org/wiki/List_of_Everton_F.C._seasons

41. Readytogo.net – 'English Football Clubs Average Attendance History?' 31.07.13

42. Thomas John Preston – 'The origins and development of Association Football in the Liverpool district, c. 1879 until c.1915' 2007 University of Central Lancashire

43. David Kennedy – *A Social and Political History of Liverpool and Everton Football Clubs: The Split 1878-1914* 2017 Routledge

44. David Kennedy, op. cit.

45. David Kennedy, op. cit.

46. David Kennedy, op. cit.

47. David Kennedy, op. cit.

48. Peter Lupson – 'How Everton Came to Move' 25.01.2017 Evertonfc.com/news

49. David Kennedy and Michael Collins – 'Community Politics in Liverpool and the Governance of professional football in the late nineteenth century' *The Historical Journal* 2006 Cambridge University Press

50. David Kennedy and Michael Collins, op. cit.

51. David Kennedy and Michael Collins, op. cit.

52. Tony Mason, op. cit.

53. David Kennedy – *A Social and Political History of Liverpool and Everton Football Clubs: The Split 1878-194* 2017 Routledge

54. James Corbett – Everton the School of Science 2004 Pan MacMillan

55. Tony Mason, op. cit.

Chapter 2

1. Dod – 'Trouble Between Orange Bigots and Liverpool people' September 2007 Politics.ie forum

2. David Kennedy – 'Red and Blue and Orange and Green?' 31.01.2010 ToffeeWeb

3. Laura Kelly – 'Irish Migration to Liverpool and Lancashire in the Nineteenth Century' 2014 University of Warwick

4. Laura Kelly, op. cit.

5. 'Liverpool: Trade, population and geographical growth' British History Online

6. British History Online, op. cit.

7. John Simkin – 'Liverpool' – September 1997 Spartacus Educational

8. David Kennedy – 'The division of Everton Football Club into hostile factions: the development of professional football organisation on Merseyside, 1878-1914' 2003 University of Leeds

9. Andrew Lees – *The Hurricane Port: A Social History of Liverpool* 2011 Mainstream Publishing

10. David Kennedy – 'Red and Blue and Orange and Green?' 31.01.2010 ToffeeWeb

11. Frank Neal – *'Sectarian Violence: The Liverpool Experience 1819-1914'* 2003 Newsham Press

12. Independent.ie 'Rooney is part of a generation Irish 'on the inside' ' – 11.10.2006

13. David Kennedy – 'Red and Blue and Orange and Green?'
    31.01.2010 ToffeeWeb

14. David Kennedy, op. cit.

15. Dod – 'Trouble Between Orange Bigots and Liverpool people'
    September 2007 Politics.ie forum

16. John Williams – Into the Red Liverpool FC and the Changing
    Face of English Football 2001 Mainstream Sport

17. Dod – 'Trouble Between Orange Bigots and Liverpool people'
    September 2007 Politics.ie forum

18. Paddy Shennan – 'Cilla and Ricky's "Scouseness" Test!' 17.12.
    2002 Liverpool Echo

19. Tommy Smith – *I Did It the Hard Way* p.14. 1981
    Readers Union

20. J. P. Dudgeon – Our Liverpool: Memories of Life in
    Disappearing Britain 2010 London: Headline Review

21. David Kennedy – *A Social and Political History of
    Liverpool and Everton Football Clubs: The Split 1878-1914*
    2017 Routledge

22. John Belchem – *Irish, Catholic and Scouse – The
    History of the Liverpool-Irish 1800-1939* 2007 Liverpool
    University Press

23. David and Peter Kennedy – Irish Football Clubs in Liverpool
    16.09.17 Amazon

24. David and Peter Kennedy, op. cit.

25. David and Peter Kennedy, op. cit.

26. David and Peter Kennedy, op. cit.

27. John Belchem – *Irish, Catholic and Scouse – The
    History of the Liverpool-Irish 1800-1939* 2007 Liverpool
    University Press

28. Bill Murray – *The Old Firm: Sectarianism, Sport and Society
    in Scotland* 1984 John Donald Publishing

29. Bill Murray, op. cit.

30. Bill Murray, op. cit.

31. The Newsroom – 'The Old Firm story: How sectarianism came to define a derby' 01.07.16 *The Scotsman*

32. Stephen F. Kelly – *The Kop* 1993 Mandarin

33. Bill Murray – The Old Firm: Sectarianism, Sport and Society in Scotland 1984 John Donald Publishing

34. Keith Daniel Roberts – 'The rise and fall of Liverpool sectarianism' 04.15 University of Liverpool

35. Belfast Celtic Society – 'The History of the Grand Old Team'11.02.2019

36. Eamonn McCann – 'The day a team died' 07.08.17 *Sunday Tribune*

37. David and Peter Kennedy – *Irish Football Clubs in Liverpool* 16.09.17 Amazon

38. Michael Kenrick – 'Are Evertonians Catholic or Protestant?' 2004 ToffeeWeb

39. David Kennedy – 'Red and Blue and Orange and Green?' 31.01.2010 ToffeeWeb

40. Peter Lupson – *Thank God for Football!* 2006 Azure

41. IBWM – 'Manchester United: A Lifetime on the Left' 06.09.12

42. Stuart Brennan – 'Why Rangers 'hate' the Reds' 12.08.04 Manchester Evening News

43. Victor Martins – 'Is Manchester United Catholic or Protestant?' 11.08.20 FootballPredictions.NET

44. Brian James – Journey to Wembley 1977 Marshall Cavendish

45. Andrew O'Hagan – 'The final whistle for God's squad?' 27.02.99 The Guardian

46. Keith Daniel Roberts – 'The rise and fall of Liverpool sectarianism' 04.15 University of Liverpool

47. Keith Daniel Roberts, op. cit.

48. Keith Daniel Roberts, op. cit.

49. Glasgow City Council – 'Sectarianism in Glasgow – Final Report' January 2003

50. Keith Daniel Roberts – 'The rise and fall of Liverpool sectarianism' 04.15 University of Liverpool

51. Keith Daniel Roberts, op. cit.

52. Keith Daniel Roberts, op. cit.

53. David Kennedy – 'Red and Blue and Orange and Green?' 31.01.2010 ToffeeWeb

54. Tony Mason – 'The Blues and the Reds– A History of the Liverpool and Everton football clubs' 1985 The History Society of Lancashire and Cheshire

55. Rob Sawyer – 'St. Luke's – the Church with its own Football Stadium!' 05.01.18 efcheritagesociety.com

56. Andrew Lees – *The Hurricane Port: A Social History of Liverpool* 2011 Mainstream Publishing

57. Andrew Lees, op. cit.

58. Keith Daniel Roberts – 'The rise and fall of Liverpool sectarianism' 04.15 University of Liverpool

59. 59. Brick_Top – 'To hell with Liverpool and Rangers too – Everton song' 23.10.20 www.followfollow.com

Chapter 3

1. Attendance History. ToffeeWeb. Retrieved 2 November 2009

2. P. Kirkbride – 'Everton announce season tickets sold out for next term' 02.06.17 *Liverpool Echo*

3. 'The F. A. Premier League National Fan Survey Report 2004/05' Premier League

4. 'The F. A. Premier League National Fan Survey Report 2007/08' Premier League

5. Liverpool Echo – 'So how local are our club's fans?' 05.03.02 Liverpool Echo

6. Matthew Taylor – Football A Short History 2011 Shire Publications

7. Hammersmith and Fulham Council – 'Parsons Green and Walham Ward Profile 2018' 2018

8. Alasdair Rae – 'Under the raedar' 09.11.15 undertheraedar.com

9. Liverpool City Council – 'The Index of Multiple Deprivation 2019: A Liverpool analysis' 2019

10. Wikipedia – 'Everton F. C. supporters'. Retrieved June 2020

11. LiverpoolExpress – 'Deprivation Factfile' 08.10.19 LiverpoolExpress

12. 'The F. A. Premier League National Fan Survey Report 2003/04' Premier League

13. Vivek Chaudhary – 'Football's profile is white and wealthy' 27.02.02 The Guardian

14. George Bond – 'Highest earning Premier League fans revealed...' 02.08.18 The Sun

15. 'The F. A. Premier League National Fan Survey Report 2002/03' Premier League

16. Zoopla – 'Zoopla reveals 2012 Property Premier League' 16.08.12 Zoopla

17. Gabriel M. Ahlfeldt and Georgios Kavetsos – 'Form or Function? The Impact of New Football Stadia on Property Prices in London' 2011 London School of Economics

18. Jelmer de Visser – 'The impact of a full Premier League-takeover on house prices' 04.03.21 Rijksuniversiteit Groningen

19. Jelmer de Visser, op. cit.

20. This is Anfield – 'Reds outnumber Blues 2-to-1 in Liverpool, says Everton's own report' 21.02.20

21. Liverpool Echo – 'Everton ride high in Premier League fan satisfaction survey' 17.03.15 Liverpool Echo

22. Matthew Taylor – Football A Short History 2011 Shire Publications

23. LiverpoolExpress – 'Everton in the Community Granted Freedom of the City' 08.05.18 Liverpool City Council

24. Henry Winter – 'Everton are a shining beacon for football as a force for good in the community' 10.01.15 The Telegraph

25. Henry Winter – 'Everton tackling social issues with 'power of badge' ' 04.03.19 The Times

26. Henry Winter, op. cit.

27. LiverpoolExpress – 'Everton in the Community Granted Freedom of the City' 08.05.18 Liverpool City Council

28. 'Everton in the Community saved my life' 14.05.19 Premier League

29. David Prentice – 'Fan says, "Everton saved my life" and now intends to give something back' 19.11.21 *Liverpool Echo*

30. David Collins – 'Everton stars talk away the blues with isolated fans' 24.01.21 *The Times*

31. 'Community contribution' 2021 https:// premierleague.com

32. David Conn – 'Everton show the way by promoting community rather than gambling' 10.02.20 *The Guardian*

33. 'Cazoo pledges up to £50,000 to support Everton in The Community' 17.09.20 www.cazoo.co.uk

34. Mark Critchley – 'Everton sponsors make second social media gaffe by describing club as a 'hopeless place' ' 22.11.17 *Independent*

35. Charlie Parker-Turner – '15 Premier League and EFL clubs who need to change shirt sponsors after betting ban' 23.09.21 *Mirror*

36. Adam Jones – 'Everton urged to turn back on gambling sponsor as thousands sign petition' 29.06.22 *Liverpool Echo*

37. TheGuide Liverpool – 'New Everton in the Community mental wellbeing hub receives big funding boost' 09.02.22

38. Liverpool Echo – 'Everton ride high in Premier League fan satisfaction survey' 17.03.15 *Liverpool Echo*

39. GrandOldTeam – 'Everton Fan Survey 2018/19' 30.05.19 It's a GrandOldTeam to Support

40. Paul MacDonald – 'Revealed: The Teams with the Most Dangerous Wages-to-Revenue Ratio' 07.07.20 footballcritic.com

41. Simon Hart – 'Everton fans cautious but upbeat for new dawn as Farhad Moshiri buys 49.9 per cent stake in club' 28.02.16 *Independent*

42. Simon Hart – 'Everton's 'family' feud over lack of funding in transfers and Goodison Park' 25.08.15 *Independent*

43. Adam Jones – 'Farhad Moshiri confirms Rafa Benitez stance with text message after Everton derby defeat' 02.12.21 *Liverpool Echo*

44. David Prentice – 'Everton's best ever results in independent Premier League fans survey' 18.03.21 *Liverpool Echo*

45. Jack Pitt-Brooke and Martin Hardy – 'Fan power: Hull City, Bolton and Everton among clubs to see supporters making their voices heard in the board room' 08.10.13 *Independent*

46. James Corbett – *Everton the School of Science* 2010 deCoubertin Books

47. James Corbett, op. cit.

48. Matt Jones – 'Everton-or-Liverpool-FC-more-popular-in-Liverpool' 13.01.19 Quora

49. David Kennedy –'Football stadium relocation and the commodification of football: The case of Everton supporters and their adoption of the language of commerce' May 2012 *Soccer and Society* vol. 13 no. 3

50. Hamish Champ – 'Everton FC to launch new stadium consultation' 25.10.18 Building

51. Hamish Champ, op. cit.

52. Phil Kirkbride – 'Everton win major public support for new Bramley-Moore Dock stadium plans as consultation results revealed'13.11.19 Liverpool Echo

53. Stephen Chapman – 'Everton stadium campaign praised by academics and marketers' 19.09.19 Prolific North

54. Phil Kirkbride – 'Everton's consultation over new stadium at Bramley-Moore Dock wins award' 22.11.19 *Liverpool Echo*

55. 'Public consultation for new Everton stadium wins national planning award for engagement' 09.09.20 The People's Project www.peoplesproject.co.uk

56. ' 'No' to Olympic Stadium move' 14.05.12 Football Supporters' Association

57. Anthony Kelly – 'Why Everton need to avoid the sad mistakes made by West Ham in pursuit of new stadium' 19.12.19 thefootballfaithful.com

58. Bob Waterhouse – 'Survey of Westcountry Blues' 20.01.18

59. 'The F. A. Premier League National Fan Survey Report 2007/08' Premier League

60. Emilia Bona – 'The women of Goodison: the story of Everton's unique bond with female fans' 03.08.18 Liverpool Echo

61. Gail J. Newsham – *In a League of Their Own! The Dick, Kerr Ladies 1917-1965* 1994 Paragon

62. Paul Brown and Vivek Chaudhary – 'Everton fans top racist 'league of shame' ' 07.01.00 *The Guardian*

63. Bradley Cates – 'Everton and Racism' 27.0.17 EFC Statto

64. Paul McNamara – 'Everton Pair on Reaction if a Player Revealed he was Gay' 25.07.20 https://www.evertonfc.com/news

65. Daniel Zeqiri – 'Revealed: The Premier League fanbase most in favour of Brexit...and the fans who regret their vote' 28.09.17 The Telegraph

66. Paul Taylor – 'Everton: Which way did fans vote on Brexit?' 01.10.17 Fansided princerupertstower.com

67. BBC News – 'EU referendum: Merseyside split on Brexit' 24.06.16

68. Liverpool Echo – 'So how local are our clubs' fans' 05.03.02 *Liverpool Echo*

69. 'The Premier League Social Network Rankings' 2019 newtoninsight.net

70. Wikipedia – 'Everton F. C. supporters'

71. 'The Premier League Social Network Rankings' 2019 newtoninsight.net

72. Stephen Chapman – 'Everton ramps up marketing in America following Rodriguez arrival' 10.09.20 Prolific North

73. Sam Carroll – 'James Rodriguez, Everton pre-season plans and the 6000% shirt sale increase in Colombia' 17.03.21 *Liverpool Echo*

74. Everton – 'Everton Reveals Next Stage of International Strategy' 15.04.21 Evertonfc.com

75. David France, Rob Sawyer, and Darren Griffiths – *'Toffee Soccer Everton and North America'* 2021 deCoubertin Books

76. David France, Rob Sawyer, and Darren Griffiths, op. cit.

77. Alex Dimond – 'Everton's Devoted US Fans on Their Passion for the Club' 04.02.15 bleacherreport.com

78. Everton Forum – 'Everton USA Supporters Clubs – Everton in America' https://theevertonforum.co.uk

79. Dave Powell – 'Everton land new commercial deal to target major market' 02.12.21 *Liverpool Echo*

80. Louise Taylor – 'Number of overseas fans at Premier League games rises to 800,000' 10.09.15 *The Guardian*

81. VisitBritain Research – 'International Buzzseekers Football Research' June 2019 visitbritain.org

82. VisitBritain Research, op. cit.

83. Cameron Easley – ' 'Global Is Cool': The Growing Appeal of Premier League Soccer in America' 28.08.19 morningconsult.com

84. Bob Waterhouse – 'Survey of Westcountry Blues' 20.01.18

Chapter 4

1. Ulrich Beck – *What is Globalization?* Cambridge; Polity press 2000

2. Jean François Lyotard – *La Condition Postmoderne* Les Éditions de Minuit

3. Nigel Watson – 'Postmodernism and lifestyles' in Stuart Sim – The Routledge Companion to Postmodernism 2005 Routledge

4. Bruno Pantaleoni – 'Football Beyond Borders: How Clubs Expand to New Markets' Sports Business Institute Barcelona sbibarcelona.com

5. Samuel Granados – 'A football story How big money remade the people's game' 25.05.21

6. ToffeeWeb – 'Attendance History' toffeeweb.com/history/ records/attendances.asp

7. Simon Inglis – *The Football Grounds of Great Britain* 1987 Collins Willow

8. Joel Sked – 'The evolution of the football fan – and what it says about the game' 05.09.17 inews.co.uk

9. BBC News – 'Did the 1966 World Cup change England?' BBC News 24.07.16

10. BBC News, op. cit.

11. Richard Foster – '1966: what you might not know about the most famous year in English football' 11.02.16 *The Guardian*

12. James Cleary – *Everton The Official Autobiography* 2012 Sport Media

13. Joel Sked, op. cit.

14. Transalpino – Everton v Millwall 1973 (Liverpool Echo) The day Millwall tried to take the St End, Bizarrely Liverpool were at home to city across the park at the same time. https:// www.facebook.com/transalpinoliverpool/photos/everton-v-millwall-1973

15. FW Admin, Football Whispers – 'Stairway to Hell: The Ibrox Disaster of January 2 1971' Footballwhispers.com

16. Simon Inglis – *The Football Grounds of Great Britain* 1987 Collins Willow

17. Neil Cameron – 'Rangers couldn't ignore how their support has changed' *The Herald* 24.07.19

18. Jon Henderson – 'Staying away days' 16.03.03 *The Guardian*

19. Martin Fletcher – *Fifty-Six: The Story of the Bradford Fire* 2015 Bloomsbury

20. Steve Greenfield and Guy Osborn Football Fans and the Law – 'After the Act? The (re)construction and regulation of football fandom' 24.03.2010 Urban75

21. Ed Vulliamy – 'Heysel stadium disaster: 'I saw the rows of bodies piled high' ' 27.05.15 *The Guardian*

22. The Sunday Times – 'Putting the boot in' 19.05.1985 *The Sunday Times*

23. Simon Inglis – 'A brief history of the Hillsborough disaster and justice campaigner Anne Williams' April 2020 History Extra

24. Dave Page – 'A Brief History and Overview of the English Premier League' www.streetdirectory.com

25. Matthew Taylor – *The Association Game: A History of British Football* 2013 Routledge

26. BBC News – 'The Men who Changed Football' 10.02.01 BBC News

27. Paul MacInnes – 'Deceit, determination and Murdoch's millions: how Premier League was born' 23.07.17 *The Guardian*

28. Paul MacInnes, op. cit.

29. Paul MacInnes, op. cit.

30. Joshua Robinson and Jonathan Clegg – *The Club How the Premier League Became the Richest, Most Disruptive Business in Sport* 2018 John Murray

31. Eoin Connolly – 'The rights track: a history of the Premier League's UK TV deals' 13.02.18 sportspromedia.com

32. Alex Christian – 'Amazon's Boxing Day football bonanza could totally reshape the Premier League' 26.12.19 Wired

33. Premier League – 'Interacting with a global audience' premierleague.com

34. Christopher Atkins – 'How the UEFA Champions League Changed World Football' 08.04.13 bleacherreport.com

35. Stefan Szymanski – 'The future of football in Europe' 17.01.07 Penn State Law

36. Max Kraidelman – 'The Super Bowl Is No Match For The UEFA Champions League' 05.06.15 Vocativ

37. David Lange – 'UEFA Champions League rights revenue by sector 2018/19' statista.com

38. Steve Tongue – 'Why fans struggle to feel at home with foreign owners' 10.02.13 Independent

39. Alfie Potts Harmer – '7 Football Clubs That Own Other Clubs' 2018 HITC hitc.com

40. Wikipedia – 'List of feeder teams in football'

41. Jack Kiely – 'Explainer: Who owns each of the 20 Premier League clubs?' 04.05.21 Extra.ie sport

42. Ritchie Slack – 'What comes next for FSG and Liverpool?' 24.04.21 Sports Illustrated

43. Will Pugh – 'Stanning Views – Arsenal owner Stan Kroenke's amazing £500m ranch is largest in USA and bigger than New York and LA combined' 08.02.22 *The Sun*

44. David Conn – 'Premier League ticket prices defy the very culture that built the game' 28.07.14 *The Guardian*

45. Fever Pitch – *The Rise of the Premier League* 13.09.21 BBC Two

46. fcbusiness – 'UK fans pay the most in Europe to follow the beautiful game according to research into the true cost of following football' 2018

47. Everton FC – 'Everton Freezes Season Ticket Prices for Fifth Consecutive Season' 03.12.19 evertonfc.com

48. 90min Staff – 'Ranking the Average Prices of Premier League Club's Season Tickets Ahead of 2019/20 Season' 04.07.19 90min.com

49. Michael Skey – 'Theorizing Football Fandom: Reflections on the UK and Africa' in Edith Noriega – 'Rise of Premier League globally has changed local face of fans' 18.06.18 Global Sport Matters

50. Philip Buckingham – 'What is a Premier League football fan in 2021?' 19.10.21 The Athletic

51. Nicholas Mendola – 'New fan's guide to finding favorite Premier League club' 10.08.18 NBCSports soccer. nbcsports.com

52. Jeff Snyder – 'Why You Should Support Liverpool FC' 12.12.14 32 Flags

53. Jon Davey – 'How do you decide which football team to support as a neutral?' 14.09.21 *The Guardian*

54. Jon Davey, op. cit.

55. Tamás Dóczi and András Kálmán Tóth – 'Football Fandom in England: Old Traditions and New Tendencies' *International Quarterly of Sport Science 2009/2*

56. Ferdinand Tönnies – 'Gemeinschaft and Gesellschaft' 1887 Leipzig

57. Joty Saraswati – 'Monopoly' Sociology in London – 'Football – Working-class or Middle-Class?' 11.11.18 sociologylondon. wordpress.com

58. Sociology in London – 'Football – Working-class or Middle-Class?' 11.11.18 sociologylondon.wordpress.com

59. Brian Oliver – 'How football's working-class fans were sold out for a fistful of popcorn' 18.09.16 *The Guardian*

60. 60. Samuel Granados – 'A football story How big money remade the people's game' 25.05.21

61. Brian Beard – 'Foreign Ownership of Premier League Clubs' 30.04.20 MFF myfootballfacts.com

62. Chris Knight – 'Finance expert explains why Newcastle have £205m transfer cushion to make major new signings' ChronicleLive 11.10.21

63. Louise Taylor – 'Newcastle set sights on trophies after Saudi-backed takeover ends Ashley era' 07.10.21 *The Guardian*

64. Louise Taylor, op. cit.

65. Alistair Magowan – 'How Newcastle can follow Man City to build a superclub in six steps' 17.10. 2021 BBC Sport

66. Alistair Magowan, op. cit.

67. Simon Bajkowski – 'How Man City takeover has changed the club's fanbase and Manchester' *Manchester Evening News* 08.09.2018

68. David Prentice – 'Everton's best ever results in independent Premier League fans survey' 18.03.21 *Liverpool Echo*

69. Peter Thal Larsen and Andrew Grice – 'Murdoch's Man Utd bid blocked' 10.04.99 *Independent*

70. Fever Pitch – *The Rise of the Premier League* October 2021 BBC Two

71. 71. Fever Pitch – *The Rise of the Premier League* 13.09.21 BBC Two

72. Associated Press – 'Man United Fans' Protest and Their History of Conflict With the Glazers' 03.05.21 si.com

73. FCUM – 'A History of FC United of Manchester' fc-utd.co.uk

74. Sabyasachi Roy – 'The Story of Manchester United to FC United of Manchester' 20.06.18 sportskeeda.com

75. David Conn – 'FC United of Manchester: the success story that proves what fans can achieve' 26.05.15 *The Guardian*

76. Greg Probert – '5 Reasons Chelsea Fans Should Be Thankful for Roman Abramovich' 06.09.12. bleacherreport.com

77. James Robson – 'Thomas Tuchel at Chelsea FC helm shows brutal Roman Abramovich can conquer Europe again' 19.03.21 *Evening Standard*

78. James Robson, op. cit.

79. Declan Ahern – 'The changing face of football consumption' 15.05.20 linkedin.com

80. Martyn Ziegler – 'America falls for Premier League with £1.1 billion TV-deal scramble' 05.11.21 *The Times*

81. Martin Ziegler – 'Top clubs will get bigger slice of Premier League's new TV pie' 20.11.21 *The Times*

82. Felicia Pennant – 'Why There's No Better Time To Be A Female Football Fan' 08.06.19 *Vogue*

83. WGP Global – 'Why Women's Football Is The Fastest Growing Sport In The World'.

84. Molly Hudson – 'Ban forced women to travel globe for acclaim' 04.12.21 *The Times*

85. Dick, Kerr Ladies – 'The FA Ban' dickkerrladies.com

86. Editorial 'The Guardian View on women's football: the new deal is a gamechanger' 23.03.21 *The Guardian*

87. Damola Odeyemi – 'WSL television deal: A huge step forward for Women's football in England' 15.05.21 *Varsity*

88. Goal – 'Rapinoe slams English football for 'disgraceful' under-investment in women's game' 09.11.20 Goal.com

89. Premier League – 'Girls Football' https//www. premierleague.com

90. Martha Kelner – 'Brighton to offer free sanitary products to female fans in Premier League first' 29.08.18 *The Guardian*

91. Watford FC Staff – 'News: Women Of Watford Supporters' Group Launched' 08.06.21 Watford FC

92. Becky Morton – 'Sarah Everard: How Wayne Couzens planned her murder' 30.09.21 BBC News

93. Watford FC Staff, op. cit.

94. BBC News – ' 'More diverse' crowds at Premier League football' 25.08.10 BBC News

95. Kick It Out – 'About Us' – www.kickitout.org

96. FA Staff – 'A Statement On The Black Lives Matter Campaign In Football' www.thefa.com

97. Premier League – 'Premier League No Room For Racism Action Plan Commitments' 31.03.21 www.premierleague.com

98. Jacob Steinberg – 'From parks to the Premier League: the shocking scale of racism in English football' 12.04.19 *The Guardian*

99. Wikipedia – 'Gay Football Supporters Network' – LGBT info. Wiki

100. Helen Rumbelow – 'Football's more fun' *The Times* 06.12.21

101. Mike Henson – 'Homophobia in football: How LGBT fans' groups are changing opinions on terraces' 17.08.17 BBC Sport

102. PP Staff – 'A Brief History Of Paddy Power's Rainbow Laces Campaign' 05.09.14 https://news.paddypower.com/

103. Stonewall – 'Rainbow Laces – Let's make sport everybody's game' 2021 www.stonewall.org.uk

104. Stonewall, op. cit.

105. Other Media Ltd – 'Best in Class: Sports Fan Engagement' other. media

106. Frankie Weaver – 'How has football changed the game on social media?' 13.11.18 sookio.com

107. Frankie Weaver, op. cit.

108. Dr. Alex Fenton – 'Social Media, Sports clubs & fan engagement' 08.08. 20 alexfenton.co.uk

109. Mark Townsend – 'Footballers and clubs to boycott social media in mass protest over racist abuse' 24.04.21 *The Guardian*

110. Ben Ellery, Callum Jones, and Steven Swinford – 'American-style European Super League was planned in secret for years' 21.04.21 *The Times*

111. Everton Football Club – 'Statement From The Board' 20.04.21 evertonfc.com

112. Phil Kirkbride – 'Barcelona legend Gerard Pique makes Everton claim about European Super League plan' 21.04.21 *Liverpool Echo*

113. Matt O'Connor-Simpson – 'Why the planned Super League collapsed' 21.04.21 www.90min.com

114. James Brownsell – 'Is this the tipping point for football fan power?' 04.05.21 Al Jazeera

115. Rupert Cornwell – 'The US franchise system...coming to a league near you?' 25.10.11 Independent

116. James Brownsell, op. cit.

117. Philip Buckingham – 'What is a Premier League football fan in 2021?' 19.10.21 The Athletic

118. David Hytner, Andy Hunter, and Jamie Jackson – 'All Premier League clubs quit Super League after FA ban warning' 20.04.21 *The Guardian*

119. David Hytner, Andy Hunter, and Jamie Jackson, op. cit.

120. 120. Matt Lawton – 'Elite teams face transfer-tax' 25.11.21 *The Times*

Conclusion

1. Phil McNulty – 'Which is the Premier League's biggest club?' 11.01.13 BBC Sport

2.   Everton Fan Map – EvertonFC.com News 2015

3.   Everton in the USA on Twitter

4.   Rodger Armstrong – 'The Blue Half Podcast:- Season 2 Episode 29' 31.03.21 rodgerarmstrong.com

5.   Nick Tyrrell – 'Plans for boutique hotel opposite site of new Everton stadium approved' 06.04.21 *Liverpool Echo*

6.   Richard Fay – 'Manchester United named as world's most popular football club' 17.08.2019 *Manchester Evening News*

SPORT

9 781739 106102